# JOURNEY OF LOVE

## A Formula for Mastery and Miracles

by Alan Mesher

A QUARTUS BOOK
distributed by

ARNAN PUBLISHING
Austin, Texas

Arnan Publishing
P.O. Box 26683
Austin, Texas 78755

Cover design by Claudia Raun

International Standard Book Number 0-942082-01-X

For my grandparents whose hearts have always
been lit by the flame of Love.

# Table
# Of
# Contents

# PART I
## Introduction
## The
## Journey
## Begins

# Chapter One

## The
## Door
## Opens

*"The transformative process, however alien it may seem at first, soon feels irrevocably right. Whatever the initial misgivings, there is no question of commitment once we have touched something we thought forever lost—our way home."*

> Marilyn Ferguson
> *The Aquarian Conspiracy*

*Why does everyone like the Tao so much at first? Isn't it because you find what you seek and are forgiven when you sin?*
*Therefore, this is the greatest treasure of the universe.*

> Lao Tzu
> *Tao-Te-Ching*

I did not choose this calling, it chose me. Who would want to be a medium, anyway? If you were brought up in Boston and oriented towards academic pursuits, being a medium meant you held seances and rapped on tables and called on phony spirits. Who would want to be an outcast, a pariah? Not me.

This story begins shortly after my graduation from Hobart College, at which time I was planning to be either a lawyer or a professor. As destiny had it, however, I awakened late for the law boards with only twenty minutes to travel twenty miles. I burst out of bed in a dazed panic, threw cold water on my face and clothes on my back, and thundered down the stairs. Once outside, I tripped on the sidewalk, fell into my car, and raced off. I was half awake, quite crazed, and driving much too fast through a series of small, sleepy, upstate New York towns.

Actually, I was doing fine until I ran three consecutive red lights. At the third light, a state trooper, having his morning coffee and donut, saw my yellow bomber fly by, and choked on his cruller. He caught me five miles down the road. Before he could get out of his car, I leaped out of mine and told him I had no time to talk to him. However, I went on in authentic urgency, if he quickly took down my license number, I would appear at the state police barracks the next morning to pay my fine. He was too stunned to believe my audacity and too slow and amazed to be insulted. I jumped back in my car and roared off down the road.

I arrived without further incident at the center where the law boards were scheduled. (God must surely protect all fools and idiots, and I am one.) I was ten minutes late and frantic. The very circumspect young lady administering the exam kindly informed me in the politest of tones, that under no circumstances would I be allowed to take the exam. Not only, she said, would I be doing myself a disservice by starting late, but also I would be distracting the people taking it now. "Oh but . . ." No buts. And she cooly and gracefully turned away to other more pressing matters. I slunk off to my car, awash in self-pity. Driving home, I stayed within the speed limit, stopped at all red lights, even stop signs. I was the model of contrition and penance.

On Sunday, my bad habits and bad luck persisted, leading me to think the two were inexorably linked. I overslept again, although I had agreed to be at the police barracks at 9:30 a.m. that Sunday morning. At 10:30 a.m., I was awakened by a hard rapping, a strong tapping, on my chamber door. I threw on my clothes and stumbled to the door. In the hot summer sunlight stood two six-foot-five state troopers. Beyond them in the street were two police cruisers and an entire neighborhood of excited children and whispering parents.

In those days, I lived in an old Italian neighborhood where everyone had a garden in the backyard. Order, decency, respect for the neighbors and the law were the unspoken code of the neighborhood. Yesterday I had broken the speeding law; but today I violated the territorial imperative. First a fine and now censure.

I invited the troopers in for a cup of coffee. They agreed and I closed the door on the disapproving world. The officer with whom I had been so abrupt and rude the morning before wrote me a ticket for speeding 10 m.p.h. beyond the legal limit, which he accompanied with a verbal warning to get out of the state—fast. Since I was leaving the next week anyway, I agreed.

I spent that summer after college graduation touring Europe, debating the pros and cons of registering once more for the law boards, and promising myself that if I registered for the exam again, I would arrive on time. My internal debate proved to be idle speculation. When I returned to the states, I accepted a job teaching American history in a suburban Boston high school, in effect ending my law career.

Since this was the high school I had attended as a student, my former teachers were suddenly transformed into colleagues. According to the dictates of the head of my department, I was to "instruct" my pupils in the Compromise of 1820, the Civil War and the Great Depression. My job was to drill these indisputable facts of American history into the "beasts" and test them. I was to be tough and stern and model my style of teaching on hers. I tried. I had to. She would have made General Patton shudder. My students, however, couldn't have cared less. The more I struggled with her "tried and true formula," the more time I spent disciplining them.

In desperation I changed my style and ventured into the unknown. Once a week, I had them lay aside their books and, one by one, go to the front of the room and talk about themselves. Anyone caught putting on an act or trying to entertain or avoid revealing himself or herself was nailed immediately. I threatened them, I mocked them, I loved them. I did anything to break their facade and touch their core. The outcome of that experience was startling, yet simple. We found out that in spite of obvious differences, we were people who enjoyed being together. And that made all the difference. The kids became motivated to learn and started acting responsibly. They formed study groups, researched topics, and shared what they learned with their classmates. As I taught them to use their individuality, talents and potential, they proved they were capable and intelligent human beings.

Unfortunately, my method was neither universally accepted nor acclaimed. Not by the faculty. Not by the adminstration. Not by the parents. Time and again I was called to the principal's office to answer some new complaint lodged against me by one or another of these factions.

Collecting myself for the encounter, I would clear my throat, knock on the door, and walk in. I would say hello. The principal would be standing behind his desk. He would ask me to sit down. I would sit down, and he would sit down too. Then he would point his finger at me and shake it and say, "See here, Alan . . ." and repeat the complaint. I'd sit quietly and respectfully until he finished. Then I would say, "You know, sir, you are a good man, and you have a good heart." And he would automatically relax and slip into the past. He would put his feet up on the desk, fold his hands behind the back of his head, and reminisce about his student days at Harvard, thirty years ago. After twenty minutes of telling me the same stories in the same order, day after day, he would get up, thank me for coming in, and ask me to be sure to visit him soon. And I would say, "Well, sir, I'm sure you can count on seeing me again before the week is over." We would shake hands and I would leave.

Despite these humorous episodes, I was rapidly becoming the focal point of a gathering storm. Faculty, parents, administration and the superintendent of schools wanted my head on a platter. I didn't have much support, and I didn't like the odds. There were only two possibilities: get clobbered or get out.

When I consulted the I Ching, the Chinese book of

oracles, it advised: "As power of inferior people is growing, danger draws close to one's person; already there are clear indications of disturbed rest. Moreover, in this dangerous situation, one is yet without help or friendly advances from above or below. Extreme caution is necessary in this period of isolation. One must adjust to the time and promptly avoid the danger. Stubborn perseverance in maintaining one's standpoint would lead to downfall."

I wholeheartedly agreed. I wasn't about to be stubborn and get clobbered. I left at the end of the year. On my last day, the kids threw a surprise party for me and gave me a sweater and a homemade afghan, both of which I still have and use. We had come together for a time and touched, discovering and sharing the secret of love inside us all. Now we were each taking what had been learned and were moving on.

My first idea after leaving the teaching profession was to explore the coast of Maine and find a good place to settle. I never made it. One day while reading a Boston paper, I came across an ad for a commune starting in southern New Hampshire. The ad spoke of forty acres of land, a good, solid farmhouse, a new barn, a few cabins, cows and chickens, and a desire for two more members.

After being alone at the center of a storm in inner city Boston, the idea of the countryside with a farm and caring community sounded like heaven. From the vantage point of this earth, and its problems, heaven has always been tempting. Naturally I went.

As with most earthly attempts at heaven, however, something went awry. There is an earthly saying: "It takes all kinds." It's just like that in heaven too. This particular paradise was ruled by a petulant little boy who never grew up. When he didn't get his way, he would fly into a rage and accuse and blame and threaten. I had just left one authoritarian regime; I didn't need another. When I found that a new friend, Larry, a sculptor, was building a house a few miles away, I offered to help him complete it if I could live there in exchange.

While living at Larry's, I kept hearing strange stories about a woman named Eleanor, who possessed the abilities of spiritual healing and mystical insight. From the stories of compassion, guidance, and positive changes I heard, it was

obvious that the people who knew Eleanor loved her deeply.
I was certainly in search of a changed life. The academic
calling had failed me, or I had failed it. Where the fault lay
did not matter. I needed something deeper, something
joyous and healing. I hungered to meet Eleanor. There was
only one problem. No one would take me to her, and no one
would tell me how to find her.

During this period of frustration, I decided to see if I
could teach a yoga class at the Keene YMCA. I had been
doing yoga intensely for a year and felt it was now time to
teach it. During my year as a high school teacher, three
different students had mentioned to me during impromptu
conversations concerning the future (theirs, not mine) that I
should take up yoga, although none of them knew much
about it, much less practiced it. Why were they telling me to
do yoga? Where was their advice coming from anyhow?

One day I went home to visit my parents. I hadn't even
taken off my jacket when my mother said to me, "Alan, you
should do yoga." It's a plot, I thought, but who or what is
organizing it?

Nevertheless, the handwriting was on the wall. I started
taking yoga lessons. Soon my chronically stiff back loosened
so that I could touch my palms to the floor for the first time
in my life. I felt great and wanted to give others the same
sense of health and exhilaration I had received from yoga.
Accordingly, one early fall day, I drove into Keene seeking
employment as a yoga teacher at the YMCA.

I found the Program Director in his upstairs office, feet
propped on the desk, bouncing a volleyball off the wall. He
didn't look very approachable but nevertheless I introduced
myself and told him I would like to teach a yoga class.

"Nope," he said. "No one around here wants a yoga
class. Got no use for it. Sorry." Abrupt and to the point.
Spoken like a true Yankee.

I went back to the house in the woods and took a safe,
no-risk job with a nearby contractor. I lasted a month, then
quit and decided to try the Keene "Y" again.

The next day, I went to the "Y" and climbed the stairs.
There was no sound of a ball bouncing off the wall. Maybe he
was away, or at lunch, or in the sauna. Hardly. He was there
with his legs on the desk, his hands behind his head, and his

gaze fixed on the gym.

I cleared my throat, but not loudly, and closed the door. He looked at me absently for a few seconds and then remembered. His eyes became bright. He popped out of his chair and pumped my hand.

What the hell is going on, I thought.

"Boy, am I glad to see you. Where have you been? I've been trying to locate you for a month."

"You have?"

"Yeah. Within two weeks of your coming in last month, thirty women either called up or came by asking for a yoga class. You got yourself a job!"

"I do?"

"You do."

Twice a week thereafter, on Tuesday and Thursday mornings, I commuted to Keene and taught yoga at the YMCA. We were in a bleak gym with no windows, but it didn't matter. The classes had a warmth and loving presence of their own.

Meanwhile, the thought of meeting Eleanor never entirely went away, occurring to me more than twice a week. By now, the weather had changed. The leaves were down, dead, and buried under the mid-November snows. While living in the woods made sense in summer and fall, the advent of winter left my truck buried in drifts at the bottom of Larry's driveway—in four feet of snow, 800 feet up a steep gully, with a pitted dirt and stone road that was a summer adventure trail at best. It was three days before the town got around to plowing it. Two more days elapsed before I could get my truck up the drive and onto the road. I missed two yoga classes and made myself miserable because of it. It was obvious I needed to live closer to town and the main road.

A week later, I moved into a new house with a melancholy musician named Dick. Dick knew Eleanor and, more importantly, where she lived. Here, I thought, was my big chance. Soon after moving in, I asked Dick if he'd take me to meet her and he said no. After waiting a few more days, I approached him differently and asked for her telephone number, saying I'd call her and see if she would see me. He still said "Nope." Several days later, I asked, what if someone were really sick or suicidal, and the last recourse was Eleanor because all traditional sources of help had been exhausted. Would he get in contact with Eleanor then? "Maybe," he said.

Finally, I told him there was a severely overweight diabetic lady in my yoga class whose daughter had run away last week. When I asked him to call Eleanor and arrange for her to see this lady, he still said "Nope," and walked away. Three failures were enough for me. I had tried and tried again, but that old adage had no magic for me. I gave up trying and allowed more weeks to pass.

One evening shortly after Christmas, Dick came out of the back room with his guitar and a funny smile on his face. In addition to his old, beat-up jacket and woolen mittens, he was wearing a beret and a wool scarf. This stuck me as strange because he seldom smiled, rarely wore the beret, and never with that scarf. For the moment he was transformed; not a dour Yankee, but a jaunty musician and celebrator of life.

"I'm going over to Eleanor's," he announced.

My mouth fell open but I didn't say a thing. After sitting for a few seconds, I bolted into the hall, threw on my jacket, and leaped into the car before Dick emerged from the house, shaking his head all the way down the stairs.

There was little to see in the darkness as we drove to the town where Eleanor lived. The quarter moon hung low on the horizon barely illuminating the crowded pine trees which loomed over the road. After rounding a long turn, we came to a bog where there had been a great fire years earlier, reminding me of a time in my childhood when a definite sense of purpose, a clear vision, blazed in my heart. All of that was distant now and almost gone; there was nothing in the bog at this time except the somber skeletons of some charred trees. A few miles up the road, we saw the lights of Eleanor's town. When we arrived at her house, I didn't give Dick the honor of going first. Bounding up the icy stairs, I rang the bell.

The door opened and there was Eleanor, laughing and greeting us. She pulled us into her dark hall and, immersing us in her ample arms, hugged us both soundly. As she did so, a soft, loving energy poured into me and I felt lighter and better than I had in years.

She led us into her kitchen and sat us at her table while

she fixed a pot of tea. Then she sat down next to me and started talking. I could feel her presence suddenly leap into me. A tingling sensation, which began at the base of my spine and spread upwards, was accompanied by an inner heat that started in my hips and spread through my stomach into my heart. I felt a strange mixture of ecstasy, relaxation and peace rising inside me. I could hardly contain myself. I wanted to sing and dance and shout and embrace the whole world. It was only with great effort that I stayed in my chair. Although my eyes were riveted on Eleanor, I didn't hear a word she was saying. I was somewhere else.

Then something seemed to pop in my forehead, and for a moment I became conscious of a soft white and golden light surrounding her and pouring into me. At the same time, it seemed to fill the room. Extending a few feet from her body was a radiant, golden energy, beyond which a soft, luminous white light spread for several more feet.

After a moment, I no longer saw the light but instead grew very conscious of the quality of her voice. Her speaking had a rich, full, musical quality. The resonance and healing power in her words commanded my closer attention. She was speaking of events from my childhood, things I had long since forgotten. Now they came back to me; guided by her empathy and insight, I finally saw the pattern and understood the purpose behind the difficulties of my early years. "Alan," she said, "You are here to give. You are here to help people. You will always be in front of the public."

Everything up to that point was fine. However, the idea of being in front of the public was a little difficult to digest. On the outside, I exhibited a little false bravado: on the inside, I was hiding out.

From that night on, all I wanted was to be at Eleanor's home. I was hungry for the subtle food she fed me and managed to contrive all kinds of excuses for being in her area and "casually" dropping in. Every time I visited, I learned something new and left feeling immensely better. To the outside world, I probably appeared a trifle crazy. I found myself laughing a great deal, unable to stay sad, serious or depressed for long. I felt free of things that had burdened me for years. One night I had a dream of spring flowers blooming and a great mantle of spring leaves budding on the maples near my window. The dream symbolized my inner transformations. The years of conditioning and repression, of trying to be what I wasn't, were coming unraveled, and the real me, inside and choking for so long, was waking.

A few weeks later, a reporter from the *Keene Sentinel* called and asked if the paper could do a story on my yoga class.

"Of course," I replied, quite thrilled.

They sent a photographer to the class, and I had a long interview with the reporter. I found a picture of myself in the next Saturday's paper, sitting in a yoga posture on the middle of the front page, with an accompanying article. I didn't expect Eleanor's prophecy about being in front of the public to come true so soon.

One day when I was "dropping in" on Eleanor as usual, she had a house full of people. She chuckled and demanded, "Alan, what took you so long to get here? I've been sending for you for over an hour. I need your energy to help with the healings for these people."

"You what?" I asked, astonished. Apparently two could play this game. I had thought my plotting to be at Eleanor's whenever possible was all my doing, and now I learned she was scheming too.

When the afternoon was over and only Eleanor and I remained, she said to me, "Alan, your third eye is opening; you're healed. Now that you've developed your higher energies, you will be able to help others. Most people live in the lower energies and never experience the real joy of life. Existence is gray and hard for them, full of pain, sorrow, and problems mixed with only a little pleasure. You now know the fuller spectrum of delight, joy and love, the truer parts of life. You must share this knowing and bring others into it. If people like us hung out together all the time, we'd get so high and spaced out that we'd be little good to anyone else."

I merely nodded, jaw open, looking stupid as she went on in her musical voice. "You know, Alan, you'd better watch it. Now that you've got the high energy, funny things are going to happen to you, and you're going to see strange things."

"What?" I said, racing in paranoia to the popularly held, misconceived ideas about mysticism: ouija boards and ghosts and evil spirits and black magic, blood, curses, intonations.

She chuckled, reading my thoughts, "You'll see."

I didn't have to wait long.

Two days later, while washing the dishes, I felt a sudden prompting to go outside and walk down to the woods. Putting on my overcoat and galoshes, I headed down the slope towards the trees. Before I reached them, a very bright and large emerald green diamond appeared in front of one of the large pines that marked the edge of the woods. It glowed for several minutes before gradually engulfing me in its radiance. As I stood there, rooted in its light, I felt cool, calm, silent. Telepathically I was told that this green diamond was the actual soul of the tree and that all of nature was equally imbued and permeated by the life of the whole, of the spirit, of God. Soon it diminished in size, disappearing back into the tree from which it had emerged. When I went back to my dishes and to further speculation, I was certain of two things. First, my intuitive sense was definitely functioning. The inner prompting to seek out this experience was evidence of this. Secondly, my third eye was open. I was beginning to see beyond the physical dimensions of things. The green diamond was ample evidence of that. What was next, I wondered as I finished the dishes.

A few weeks later, I was sitting in the den on a brilliant, sun-drenched winter's afternoon, drinking a cup of tea and reading the afternoon paper. As I sipped a little tea, relaxed and scanned the front page, my eyes suddenly grew leaden with exhaustion. For no apparent reason, I felt drained of energy. The paper slid off my lap and onto the floor. As my head dropped against my right shoulder, I drifted slowly into that land of strange hieroglyphics, the subconscious world between sleeping and waking.

Soon, the hazy indistinct images grew clear, well defined and recognizable. I was on the lawn of the high school where I had taught the year before. While it was a cold, winter day outside, in my vision, it was springtime and warm. The sky was blue, the lawn green and luscious and in need of cutting. Seated around me was a group of students, many of whom I knew. We were discussing their problems and generating solutions to overcome them. While we were so engaged, I noticed a halo travelling rapidly toward us on the distant horizon. As it came closer, I could see that the halo was composed of two fiery rings, the top, a pale golden yellow and the bottom, a pale blue. The halo crackled, throwing off sparks of blue and gold light, frightening me as it moved closer. What was it? What did it want and what was it going to do?

"Do you see it?" I cried to my students. "Do you see it?" But none of them could. I raised my hands to shield my head and tried to hide, hoping it would go away. Fat chance. It settled above my head and a tremendous power started flowing through me. Every cell of my body was transformed and synchronized to a higher degree of functioning. I felt light and still and extremely clear-headed. From every pore of my body this power flowed to my students. Suddenly, there were no more problems. We all felt light and free. Pain and self-concern turned to laughter in this new light.

Suddenly, I felt a strange presence over my left shoulder. Turning, I beheld a very grey, malignant entity. He, she, or it was hitting me with a vengeful and angry energy. Although I had been having a wonderful time, I was now shaken and suddenly I found myself catapulted back to my body and normal consciousness. I jerked forward and opened my eyes. An immense amount of energy was still circulating through me and in spite of that horrible presence, I felt invigorated and inspired.

I called Eleanor and told her what had happened. She listened and laughed. "Alan," she said, "that was a good experience. It was real. It happened on the astral level of experience. You see, you are expanding and seeing 'funny things'! The blue and golden halo was the Christ mind. Because you were there to help the students overcome their problems, the Christ mind came to help you and protect you in your work with them. The entity on your left was an astral idiot who was controlling the children on a subtle level by keeping their energies focused on their pain. By doing that, he could manipulate their consciousness and keep them bound in the lower energies."

"However, the Christ mind came and helped you free them. You are now a channel for that energy, and when you do your work, it will work through you. You exited early because it is all new to you. You didn't know that in the presence of the Christ mind, the astral idiot on your left is powerless. In fact, the Christ mind will destroy him. Now you know better. Don't be afraid again. You are protected."

Well, that was good news. Two months later, I was granted another important experience. This inner vision came in the form of a dream although it was a real event on the inner planes of life. As the experience unfolded, I found myself standing by a country cottage in the warm mid-day sun. A voice spoke to me and directed me to enter the cottage. I was told that I would find a baby inside. I was to bring it outside and bathe it in a tub. Although I could not see to whom the voice belonged, the tone and timbre of it seemed familiar. I trusted it and did as I was told. I went in, brought the baby out and began to wash it in the tub. As I washed the baby, three young, insolent children appeared and tried to stop me from completing my task. Not reacting, I continued to wash the baby.

The scene then changed, and I found myself with my girl friend, Alice, on a large commercial airplane. A fellow passenger came down the aisle and sat beside us for a few minutes. He said that we were bound for Tibet and were to meet a great guru. The guru, he continued, was austere, aloof and cold. Don't worry, he went on. Just do as you are told when you get there.

Presently, we landed in Tibet. It was a cold night as we started our climb into the heart of the Himalayas. After a while, we reached a building perched in the darkness on a high mountain ledge. In the front room was a dead Chinese soldier in a casket. There was blood on the front of his uniform from his wounds. We were then led downstairs and told to sit on the floor to wait for the guru. Soon the guru appeared at the top of the stairs. He was tall, elegant and bald. He was dressed in a simple white robe. As soon as I saw him, I felt a strong and deep love for him. I ran up the stairs and threw myself at his feet, but he grabbed my shoulders and made me stand.

"Follow me," he said, "and do not look back."

We walked out of the building across a barren, wind-swept plain and up a mountain. I lost consciousness of what happened while we were on the mountain, but I regained my awareness as we were crossing the plain on the way back. I looked down at my hands. My fingers were a solid, brilliant gold and my palms were lead. "What does this mean?" I wondered silently. I heard Eleanor's voice laughing in my inner ear, responding, "Alan, the gold represents the noble truth you have been initiated into, and the lead signifies the responsibility for using that truth wisely for the highest good of all."

Then the guru stopped and beckoned Alice to join us on the plain. He joined our hands and said to Alice, "You have the light to make his burden easier, and you, my son, have the sword of justice to protect her. Now go and do your work."

I awoke feeling a great brightness, clarity and joy, a deepening of what I had experienced on the high school lawn. I immediately called Eleanor. It was eight in the morning. I was thankful she was up and told her what had happened.

"Alan," she said, "it speaks for itself. You have experienced a spiritual initiation. As you were instructed, use the energy you have been given wisely. You were conscious of so much of the experience because Alice was with you. She gives you the feminine, receptive energy you need in order to be balanced. If you were not balanced, there is no way you could be conscious of that initiation. You were not allowed to know what happened on the mountain because it is not time for you to know fully what you were given. If you did, you would tamper with it. Instead, at this time, the higher energies will move through you at their discretion, and the work will be done beyond the perimeter of your awareness. You went to Tibet because in your mind, Tibet is the home of spiritual masters. As you grow in awareness, you will realize that there are masters everywhere."

One night, some months later, I lay down to sleep. I was tired and relaxed. I closed my eyes and began to fall asleep. I never made it. School was in session again. I was catapulted out of my body. After floating above myself for a few minutes, I decided to see if I could fly. It was easy. I flew through the wall and found myself speeding over the dark New Hampshire forests at enormous speed. After awhile of out-of-the-body flight, I returned to my room and re-entered my physical self, experiencing a tingling sensation throughout my body. I was elated. Instead of being exhausted, as I had been half an hour earlier, I was now highly energized. I didn't sleep much that night, and I didn't need it. Superman is real, you know, and living inside us all.

As the cycles of my inner experiences progressed, so did the seasons of New England weather. Thinking ahead, I bought an inflatable raft to use on Dublin Lake for the lazy, humid days of late summer. When they arrived, I spent many relaxing afternoons semi-sleeping on the raft, drifting along the contours of the lake. I had one minor problem, however, in this wonderful indulgence. A hearty breeze often blew over the lake, and whenever I would wake up from a short nap, I would have to paddle furiously against the wind to return to my spot. This would happen several times in one afternoon.

One day, during a semi-awake state, I had a brainstorm. The wind had just come up and I was being blown toward the middle of the lake again. I decided to imagine my raft staying put. As I was formulating the mental image of what I wanted, I heard a voice in my mind state very clearly, "No, that is not enough. You must do it with more power." That sounded logical at the time, and I began to concentrate more intently on the image. I did this for approximately half a minute and then opened my eyes, releasing the picture. Within seconds the wind shifted. It started blowing from the opposite direction and pushed me toward the place on the lake I had imagined. Within minutes, the wind dropped me exactly where I had visualized being. I remained there, floating and amazed.

By March 1974, I had been in New Hampshire for two and a half years. I had known Eleanor for two of those years. In that time, she had healed my consciousness, raised and expanded my energy level, and opened the gates to inner exploration and development of the superconscious mind. I have not yet met her equal. Whatever I do in life is partially her doing and accomplishment.

One morning in mid-March of that year, I awoke with a strong feeling that I must move to California. It was not an impression I appreciated. My life in New Hampshire was fulfilling. The country was green and lush and quiet. I lived on the shores of Dublin Lake. Mount Monadnock, the most-climbed mountain in North America, rose from the edges of my yard. In spring, dawn would find Monadnock dressed in garments of lavender and gold, the lake quivering in quiet elegance. In winter, the land was white and still, and the lake, black and brooding. With so much beauty, who needed California? In my mind, California was the land of glitter, superficiality and spurious spiritual pursuits of questionable substance. I would never leave New Hampshire. So, of course, I left New Hampshire. But not immediately.

# Chapter Two

## Strange Encounters of Many Kinds

*It is better to follow even the shadow of the best than to remain content with the worst. And those who would see wonderful things must often be ready to travel alone.*

Henry Van Dyke
*The Story of the Other Wise Man*

*When man lacks a sense of awe, there will be disaster.*

Lao Tzu
*Tao-Te-Ching*

You would think by now I would have learned something about the power of my intuition. Hardly. I learned everything the hard way. If I had been smart, I would have left for California that April. I wasn't. I sat on my behind in New Hampshire, and that's how the trouble started.

In May, my cousin Stephen came in from Colombia, South America, to spend a few days. By the time he left, he had me almost convinced to join him in his export business and move to Bogota. After all, the idea of living in a large villa on the foothills of the Andes with a servant and a maid is fairly enticing. I thought about it and bought it—hook, line and sinker, turning my back on the "still, small voice" inside me that said, California.

Frankly, it is not such a wise thing to turn your back on that "still, small voice." Take it from me. I tried, and I know. It does not go away, it gets much louder.

After two weeks of blissful idiocy, centered on day-dreaming about exotic Latin women, I began having danger-ous, unsolicited dreams. These dreams were basically the same dream with the same theme, dreamed over and over again.

In the dream, I found myself in an airport waiting to purchase a ticket to Bogota. I would be almost to the ticket counter when a man approached me from behind, grabbed me by the shoulders and said, "I'm sorry, you cannot go to Bogota. You must go to California." Then he took me to the train station and put me on a train for California.

I dreamed this dream almost every night for two weeks. Every day I tried to forget it. And every succeeding night the same strange man grabbed me by the shoulders all over again and said, "No, you must go to California."

In the third week, the dream became more dramatic. I was no longer at an airport. Instead, I was perched on a high, steep cliff with a very long and deadly fall to the valley floor below. My strange but increasingly more familiar friend was my escort and guide. "Look how dangerous your situation is here," he said. "Going to South America would be like falling off this cliff. The end. Are you ready to meet your maker?" My knees were shaking, my tongue parched. "No," I said. "No, I'm not." The "still, small voice" had won. In September I left, by car, for California.

I landed in the city that collects all nomads, wanderers, and searchers after the Holy Grail. And that is not San Francisco, it is Santa Cruz. Once Santa Cruz was a sleepy, coastal town, but it has now evolved into a lively, commercialized resort.

For once, my timing was right. I got there in the off season and rented a motel room on the beach for twenty-five dollars a week. But now what? For a month, I wandered around waiting for God to show up and say, "My son, I am glad you have come. Please step this way and see for what great purpose I have brought you hither." But all I received was a knot in my stomach and a lot of anxiety about whether I had made a mistake in coming to California.

After that first, anxious month of drifting without direction, I accidentally (accidentally?) came upon a small, metaphysical group that was just forming. At the core of this group was a woman named Diane, who had moved to Santa Cruz from San Luis Obispo. Everyone else in the group were recent arrivals to Santa Cruz as well. I had come the farthest, from New Hampshire. The others had come from New York, Oregon, the midwest, southern California and San Jose.

At first glance, Diane, like Eleanor, appeared to be a normal, middle-class mother and housewife. But in addition to that, Diane possessed supernormal abilities. She had the capacity to withdraw the core of her being, her spirit, from her physical body and ascend to greater dimensions of light and love. As she did this, the energy in the room would shift, and everyone felt uplifted. Shortly thereafter, a master entity would manifest himself through Diane's body, further increasing the light and power already pouring into the room.

Diane was a medium, and although in my opinion that is a bad choice of words, it is the one we most easily assign for that type of talent. Diane's mediumship was not the kind of show biz nonsense or strange, scary occultism usually associated with the word. There was no seance silliness, no calling on the dead, no table rapping and no playing with ouija boards.

The presence, or master, who came through Diane identified himself as Dr. Ching Li. Ching Li was of Chinese lineage, and according to him had not incarnated on the earth plane for over seven thousand years. Ching Li was articulate, well-mannered, and manifested more power and love than I had thought possible. Of course, he wasn't human, he was superhuman. Yet he possessed a great compassion for the human condition and never seemed above us or unap-proachable. We felt that we were his equals and his friends. Indeed, he encouraged that attitude.

The Doctor was gentle and kind, but when the occasion called for it, he could be an intimidating disciplinarian. He was also funny and full of a gently mocking humor that did not hurt its target because it was filled with love, but rather revealed to the person areas in which there was room for growth.

The Doctor told us that he had brought us together for several purposes. Basically, he wanted to help us evolve on our personal paths so that we would be more capable of love and strength and clarity in helping others grow as we had grown. This included the re-awakening of our inner know-ledge of healing so we could help release our fellow sojourners from pain and confusion.

At the first four group sessions I attended, I was very frustrated. I could feel the Doctor's energies, but I could see neither these energies nor the Doctor. Many others could see him, but whatever clairvoyance I possessed in New Hamp-shire failed me in California.

At the fifth session, I arrived early and sat down on the living room floor, determined to see. I closed my eyes, relaxed, and started talking to myself. "Self," said I, "this has gone on long enough. No more. Tonight you will be centered, the visionary channel will be open, and you shall see." Soon afterwards the room filled with people. Diane came in and sat down on her customary pillow. She chatted, exchanged news and after a few minutes, closed her eyes. Strange things started happening, and I could see them— clearly. First, Diane left her physical body. This aspect of her being stood off to one side and radiated a brilliant green emerald light. Next a sphere of bright blue and silver light suddenly appeared above her head and a beam of silver light shone down from this sphere, entering Diane's body. As the light poured into her, she glowed in a beautiful, silvery phosphorescence which soon changed into the form of Ching Li, superimposed over Diane's body.

The Doctor was clad in a royal blue robe, embroidered with many gold dragons, radiant with light. Around his neck, he wore a magnificent gold medallion, in the center of which was a large, clear diamond surrounded by rubies. Underneath the simple black cap, his soft, ancient face was framed by a white, patriarchal mustache and thin goatee. His blue eyes, shining wth light, depth and love, were surrounded by delicate wrinkles, perfectly complementing the smile which glistened like sunshine on the ocean.

Suddenly, a beam of lavendar light shot out from his forehead filling the darkness, and the room was haunted with the subtle luminescence of another, greater reality. I felt a subtle coolness in the room, and looked up just in time to see many other spheres of light enter through the ceiling. Some of them were blue and silver, others were gold. They quickly took on human forms, although on a more subtle plane of energy. To the physical eye, they were invisible, but to my awakened spiritual sight, they were obvious and real. They walked through the room, touching various men and women, and as they did, light exploded around these people, relaxing and brightening their formerly solemn faces.

The Doctor, however, was only beginning. From nowhere, he manifested a group of small luminescent balls in various colors which he placed in specific areas of different persons' electromagnetic fields, or auras, as they are metaphysically called. These balls of light started glowing and pouring energy into the whole aura, causing it to become more expansive and diffused with subtler colors. Reaching deeper into his bag of tricks, the Doctor then emanated several cords of a translucent energy from his head, attaching the end of each cord to the top of someone's head in the group. Later I learned that these were telepathic connections used for stimulating someone's growth from a subconscious level. As soon as these cords were attached, a rainbow stream of colors started flowing from both sides of the Doctor's body, and passing through everyone in the group, connecting us on a subtle level. I could feel the harmony and unity in the group increase as we became part of this chain of light. Then he placed a bubble of violet light over a man and a woman sitting next to each other. Their auras merged immediately. Instead of two separate, contained energy fields, there was now only one aura of overwhelming power and beauty. Speaking in his soft, lilting Chinese accent, Ching Li then answered many personal questions.

At the time of meeting Ching Li, my custom was to meditate for a half hour in the morning. One morning soon after I had first seen the Doctor, I was in a deep meditative state when my inner vision awakened and I found myself gazing at a silver screen. Soft music was playing, and a deep, well-modulated voice said, "And now for a scene from a wonderful life." Somehow, I had found my way into the Past Life Movie Theatre. The scene unfolded. I watched as a man with curly brown hair and beard sat poised and quiet in an elegant chair on the top row of an extensive outdoor arena. People were streaming up the steps of the stadium, placing flowers beside him. I could feel the devotion and respect these people had for him and the love he felt for them in return. It dawned on me that this man was myself, in some very ancient, and largely forgotten incarnation.

It is amusing to think that in a time outside the known reaches of history, I was a king, and I am thankful to know that I seemed to have ruled morally and lovingly, directed by concern for the well-being of my people. Amen. But I am also glad it is lost and gone and may it ever so remain, for I have more to do with my time than have people offer me flowers, and so, I'm sure, do you.

This first past-life experience, however, was not an isolated, titillating episode. It opened the door to the experience of other past incarnations.

During these sessions with the Doctor, I became acquainted with an interesting woman named Karen, who occasionally came to the meetings. Karen, like Diane, possessed extranormal abilities. She could leave her body at will and travel wherever she wanted, remaining fully conscious of her adventures while her body seemingly slept.

One afternoon, I was in my motel room, trying to take a nap. As I lay there with my eyes closed, turning restlessly, my inner eye opened and I saw Karen hovering near the ceiling above me. She was smiling from ear to ear. White light was pouring from her into me. No wonder I couldn't sleep,

Karen was too busy energizing me. Then I started seeing pictures of the way that Karen and I had known each other in a past life. As the pictures rolled on in my inner "projection booth," I saw us sitting at a kitchen table in a large country house in 17th century Russia. Karen was dressed elegantly in a gray-blue silk dress, and I was wearing a full-dress military uniform. We were engaged to be married, and I was about to go off to war. Karen pleaded with me to stay with her. The more she pleaded, the more vain and intolerant I became. "Woman," I heard myself say, "stop your begging. Nagging gets you nowhere. I am going to war. I shall come back a hero and marry you." How's that for a pompous fool? I came back all right . . . in a casket.

Now we had met again, not as lovers, but as friends. Even so, Karen would get quite upset when I would leave to go home. I could never figure it out. It seemed irrational and out of character for her to act that way. Now I knew. It was the past. She carried the remembrance of that life in her subconscious, and it was still living below the surface, causing her to re-enact past behavior.

A month later, at a group session, the Doctor unexpectedly became very stern with me, warning me to curb my somewhat acerbic tongue. I was shocked. He had never acted that way with me before. I thought he must be joking. I was a nice guy. I suppose, unfortunately, that no one else knew that. The Doctor warned me that if I did not curtail my caustic tendencies, my tongue would burn until I did. Now I knew he was kidding. He was incredible, but he couldn't make that happen. No one could.

The next evening I was scheduled to speak at a Symposium on Consciousness at San Jose City College. On the way to San Jose, I was concentrating on my lecture when my tongue began feeling slightly uncomfortable. Soon it was swollen. By the time I got to San Jose my mouth was on fire. I ran into a nearby drugstore and bought several boxes of cough drops. During my lecture, I popped drop after drop into my mouth and drank glass after glass of water. Nothing relieved the pain. The audience must have thought I was a very strange man plagued by a very strange affliction.

When the next session with the Doctor began, I was still in pain. My tongue was swollen and cracked. Blisters had formed on it. I begged the Doctor to end my torment. The Doctor, however, was not moved. He acted as if he were deaf and said nothing, and was utterly indifferent. My pain continued.

One month to the day of the beginning of my agony, I was as suddenly freed from my pain as I had earlier been given it. I was sitting in my daily meditation, with my eyes closed, when my inner sight opened, and I could clearly see the area above my head. Suddenly, a fist holding a transparent thunderbolt manifested itself. Before I could comprehend what was going on, the fist jammed the thunderbolt through the top of my head and down my spine. Every cell in my body was plunged into a rampant chaos, as though I was exploding. Then, like the passing of a tropical squall, I became very light, feeling purged and purified. My tongue no longer burned. I was released.

As I looked with my inner sight at the space above my head, I saw that my "crown chakra" had expanded about eighteen inches in all directions. It was now filled with the same transparent energy as the thunderbolt, with a border of very pale green light around the chakra's edges. A slight breeze brushed by my right ear and a voice said, "This is from Eta." I was amazed. Eta was my godmother who died when I was a young boy. Apparently, she was alive and well, and watching over me from the other side. Friends are always welcome. Who cares if they are invisible.

A few weeks later, I received an invitation to speak at the same metaphysical center which had sponsored the symposium at San Jose City College. I honestly don't remember what I spoke about that night, but I can guarantee you that it was less than earthshaking. The important part of the evening occurred after my talk was over, and I was getting ready to go back to Santa Cruz. A lady approached me in a rather apprehensive state and said, "I know you can heal me. Please do a healing on me."

The Doctor had taught us how to transmit energy to help people, but I had never healed anyone of a physical ailment. Now I was faced with an urgent and hysterical demand. What should I do?

"Please," she persisted. "I know you can do it. Please try."

She was certainly insistent. I reasoned that I couldn't hurt her, and she might experience some small measure of relief. She sat down and my left hand was drawn to her lung area. My hand was about ten inches from her body. A current of energy poured down my arm, through my hand towards her chest. Soon she was laughing hysterically. Her eyes began tearing. As they did, they changed in color from a sad, dark, lusterless brown to a clear, bright amber. After a few more minutes of transmitting energy, I felt the current diminish and knew it was time to stop.

She got up and was very excited and happy. She told me that she had a lung condition for which she had been taking medication for five years. During that time, her breathing had been shallow, and she was chronically weak and tired. Now she was sure she was cured and thanked me profusely. I was a bit embarrassed and bewildered. Whatever I had done, it didn't seem to be much to me.

One day, soon after this experience, I was sitting in my morning meditation. My eyes were closed, and my attention focused inwardly, when my inner vision opened and I could clearly see everything in the room. As I looked around the room, three women, two dogs and several cats walked through the wall and came over and sat beside me. The women had paper and pens and started taking notes. The dogs curled up at my feet and the cats sat next to me on the sofa. To the physical eye, they were invisible, but to my spiritual sight, they were real. It reminded me somewhat of my first past-life experience as a king. Only here my subjects were dogs and cats and three middle-aged women. I had certainly fallen a long way from my kingly days. Who says that history is progress?

Nevertheless, I found myself communicating telepathically with the women. Whatever I thought, they would write down. I didn't think that what I was thinking was very profound, but they seemed to. After a few minutes of telepathic interchange, they got up and walked through the wall and out of the room. Apparently, they got what they came for.

A week later, I had another "drop in" appearance from the denizens of the invisible reality. After being asleep for a few hours, I awoke and found myself sitting by my sleeping physical body. A strange man, also in his etheric or invisible body, walked into my room. He was wearing a white robe and looked like an Indian swami. He had dark eyes, dark copper skin, a black beard, and long black hair. He looked to be in his late thirties. He nodded to me in a friendly gesture, as if I were an old acquaintance of his and said, "You come from the same star Krishna did. Isn't that marvelous?"

It sounded great to me. I started thinking that maybe, just maybe, I was something like the god of Indian mythology. My mind was spinning. I was very excited about my own possible greatness. After all, if it had happened once to Krishna, why not once more, to me? At that moment I was a hot-air balloon ready to rise to any level of messianic stupidity with the slightest provocation.

Then the needle of my deflation entered the room. He was bald and looked familiar, dressed in an old, tattered coarse brown robe. Around him was a beautiful lavender light which filled the darkness with its beauty. Power and peace emanated from him. He came nearer to me, and I recognized him. He was the same master who had taken me to the Himalayan mountain tops a few years earlier. This time, he certainly was an imposing figure. I was in no rush to be near him. I was too frightened. He looked sternly at me and said, "Do you think that nonsense will help you see the past, present and future?"

I felt humiliated to have my folly and immaturity made so apparent to me. All I could do was hang my head and answer, "No."

Then he said, "If you want to be able to read the past, present and future, you must gain more control over yourself."

With that final remark, the two monks left the room. I was very shaken. I jumped back into my body and woke up. I didn't sleep for the rest of the night.

Two days later, I felt compelled to go to a natural food store I rarely frequented. I didn't know what I was looking for, but after walking down the aisles, I found myself in front of the periodical rack. I picked up a magazine and opened the pages. There in front of me was a picture of the two men I had seen in my room two nights earlier. The picture had been taken around 1950. They looked exactly the same in the photograph as they had in my room that spring night of 1975. The baldheaded man was identified in the magazine as Swami Sivananda and the bearded man as Swami Satchidananda. Sivananda had been a highly respected Indian guru who died in the early '50s. There are still several centers throughout the world that carry his name and tradition. Satchidananda was Sivananda's chief disciple and had been chosen by him to carry on the guru's lineage. Sometimes the dead are more influential than the living—especially when they arrive unexpectedly to test and teach you.

Then came the big event. One day in early March, I brought my car in for a tune-up. It was a gray day, raining softly. I spent the time waiting at my friend Ron's house, overlooking the beach. We were reading and listening to classical music. Exhaustion suddenly overcame me. Ron, too, felt sleepy. He dove for the large pillow on the floor and fell asleep immediately and I lay down on the sofa and fell into that suspended state between sleeping and waking. My inner eye opened, and I watched as a young lady with curly blonde hair walked into my vision, greeted me, clapped her hands and then departed.

Soon, a series of colors began exploding on the screen of my interior vision ... first white, then silver, lavender and green. These bright, exotic colors kept repeating in faster and faster sequences. A powerful energy starting at the top of my head began flowing through my body, becoming increasingly stronger as it continued to surge through me. After a few minutes, I began to leave my physical body, feeling light and quiet as I floated above my physical self. Realizing where I was, I felt a great exuberance and a madness rising in me. I decided this was my great chance. I was going to go home, back to the source. I was going to rise and float back into the heart of God.

Sleeping Ron, however, had other ideas. At the moment I made my decision to return to the source of creation, Ron separated from his physical body and came over and laid his head on my chest. Have you ever heard of anything crazier? Here we were, out of our physical bodies, and Ron decided to lay his "invisible" head on my "invisible" chest. We then had a telepathic conversation in which I asked Ron to get off my chest. He refused, saying it was necessary that I stay where I was.

As Ron remained there, keeping me by my physical body, I began to hear a whirring noise very much like the sound of a dentist's drill. At first the whirring was a distant, undefined noise, but as I listened, it became distinct and came closer to me. Soon it became four different sounds, drilling at different points in my body. One in each ear, one in my throat, and one in the center of my forehead. I was actually having an operation! After several minutes of continued drilling, the energy abated, the drilling stopped, and I eased back into my body. Seeing that the work was complete, Ron also rejoined his physical body. When we both "woke up" Ron remembered nothing of what had happened. I filled him in on the details, and we both wondered what the experience signified.

The next evening we had a group session with Ching Li. During the break, I was sitting on the arm of Diane's sofa feeling relaxed. There wasn't a thought in my mind. My body had a rhythm of its own, and I was rocking gently back and forth. Then, for some reason, my rocking ceased and my body straightened, growing stiff and rigid. An immense power rushed into me. I was swept into a sea of brilliant whiteness. Light was everywhere, hot and intense. I broke into a heavy sweat. I could see beams of brilliant white light pouring from my eyes, moving into and filling the room. Then I was speaking and saying unfamiliar things. My voice deepened, growing round and resonant. Whatever, or whoever was speaking through me spoke with knowledge and authority. After a few minutes, it was over. The energy departed, and I returned to normal consciousness. On opening my eyes, I was somewhat disoriented and startled. Everybody else looked the same way. Diane merely looked at me and smiled. She knew what had happened. I had just become a channel.

From that time on, Diane would channel the first half of the meeting, and I would channel the second half. Over the next half year, the work escalated to the point where we were meeting four to five nights a week. To write the enchanting history of that time is the work of another volume. I would rather share two curious incidents with you.

During one particular weekend session, I was channeling

an associate of Ching Li. While the Doctor was usually
gentle, compassionate and humorous in his manifestation,
this being was powerful and direct in his appearances with
us.

During the middle of the session, a member of the group
fell asleep as he usually did whenever anything interesting
was happening. The Doctor earlier had explained Greg's
habit of going unconscious as a conflict between his rigid
belief system and the new information that contradicted his
strongly-held notions. At those moments, Greg would
choose to sleep and work out his dilemma on the astral
plane. It was easier that way. This time however, his sleeping
was not a private affair. His loud snores were like drum rolls
and interfered with the progress of the session. His wife,
Julie, became increasingly embarrassed with each succeeding
snore and asked if something might be done other than
waking him. No sooner had she asked when I felt a soft arc of
energy pour through my left hand towards Greg. Within
seconds, his snoring turned to soft, rhythmic breathing. He
slept quietly, and we completed the session with no further
interruption.

On the other occasion, I was again channeling this same
being. Two members of the group, Rob and Annie, had
invited a friend of theirs to come to the meeting. This woman
was visiting from Washington state, and this was her first
time with our group. During the course of the session, the
personage I was channeling addressed himself to this woman.

"You don't believe in the higher intelligences of the
universe, do you?" he said.

"No," she answered.

He then described in great detail her relationship with her
horse. (I didn't even know she had a horse.) Then he asked
again, "Now do you believe in the higher forces of the
universe?"

Again, she replied, "No."

There was silence. After a slow minute, I felt my left arm
move straight out from my lap where it had been resting. A
great current of energy poured from my hand in her
direction. I heard some thumps, then silence, a gasp, and
more silence, then laughter. The energy had bounced her
three feet along the floor! I felt a lot of empathy for her. She

must have felt like I did when the Doctor told me my tongue would burn, and I foolishly thought that impossible. One learns fast when being taught by personalities of greater power from a greater reality.

In November 1975, the Doctor told me that I had learned all I could from him at this particular time. He told me to rest my back, which had gone out, and then return to Boston. I was somewhat relieved to know that I was going to be given a rest from so much spiritual exertion. Two weeks later, I left for the east. As I traveled through the southwest, my back flared up. It was agony to sit in the car. As the pain increased, I could not go on. I stopped in a motel in Tucumcari, New Mexico. That night I lay in bed in pain, not knowing what to do. I finally called on the Doctor and his associates to come heal me. As soon as I had voiced my need, three beings suddenly manifested themselves in the room. They were not physical but invisible. Yet with my open sight, I could see them. They stood in a line and started sending energy through me. The energy entered through my feet and began moving up my body. I maintained consciousness for as long as I possibly could. But the energy was powerful, and after a short time I fell asleep. When I awoke, I looked at the clock and saw that only fifteen minutes had gone by since they entered the room. They were nowhere in sight. I slowly got up and tested my back. There was no pain, no stiffness. I seemed to have regained my flexibility. My whole body tingled and felt very light. I did not need much sleep that night, and I resumed my travels the next day without further interruption.

It still puzzles me who those three beings were. None of them was Ching Li. They were dressed in brilliant and luminous white robes, had blue cowls over their heads and radiated a brilliant silver radiance. They never spoke. Perhaps some day if you are in need and are lucky, you will meet them.

It was to be three years before I channeled extensively again. One day in late October 1978, I heard the voice of the Doctor in my inner ear while in meditation. It had been a long time since we were last in contact and it was refreshing to feel his energy flow into mine once again, and to let his clarity, power and love expand the scope of my being. In that moment, I wanted only to remain in the deep peace I always felt while living in his presence. The Doctor, however, wasn't a bit interested in socializing. He had other things on his mind and was all business, and very clever too.

"My good friend," he said, speaking in my inner ear, "I have been patient with you for a long time, have I not?"

"Yes," I hesitantly answered. (I didn't know where this was leading, and I wasn't sure that I would like the outcome. But I knew, however, that he would inevitably wrap me around his little finger.)

"You underwent a lot of intensive training to be a channel, didn't you?"

"Yes."

"Do you think we gave you that training only for the experience of it? Only because it was something new for you? Do you think it was only fun and games?"

"I don't know. I never thought of it like that. I didn't realize there was an obligation with it."

"There is no obligation, but there is a responsibility, as with all spiritual gifts," he said. "You have been given an important gift. You have been given certain knowledge and energies which you must use to help others. That is the point of all spiritual gifts: to give, to serve and to help. You see that, don't you?"

"Yes, of course."

"How do you feel when you use your gifts to help others?" he asked.

"I feel strong and centered and clear and loving and full of humor."

"Wouldn't you like to feel that way more often?"

"Yes."

"Good," he said. "It's time for you to bring together another group of people and let them benefit from my presence as you have."

"Well," I said, knowing I was hooked, and there was no way out, but wanting to be cautious and independent anyway. "I'll do it only if it's easy to bring a group together."

"It will be easy," he said, "Very easy."

It was.

* * *

What follows in this book is the distillation of a part of

the knowledge and information presented in these meetings. To date there have been almost two hundred meetings held in different cities including Austin and San Antonio, Texas; Palo Alto and Santa Cruz, California; Wilmington, Delaware; Boston, New York, Philadelphia, Peterboro, New Hampshire and London, U.K.

# Part II

## From
## Despair
## to
## Divinity

What is a Great Man?
A great man is driven by neither anxiety nor ambition.
He has no desire for recognition or fame. Rather, the
great man, having discovered his true nature, is filled
with Love. From this discovery, his greatness flows.

For the great man life is internally rich and peaceful.
He is content. Neither struggle nor conflict stirs within
him. Because of his contentment, his activities are filled
with clarity and compassion. This is the essence of his
greatness.

The Great Man does not want to be different from
his friends and neighbors. Rather, he wants them to be
as fulfilled as he is. This is the secret of his greatness.

# Chapter Three

# The
# First Law
# of
# Consciousness

> *Too much success is not an advantage.*
> Lao Tzu
> *Tao-Te-Ching*

> *Success is not enough.*
> Liv Ullman

> *In the pursuit of learning, every day something is acquired.*
> *In the pursuit of Tao, every day something is dropped.*
> Lao Tzu
> *Tao-Te-Ching*

## Success is Not Enough

Making life work is not an easy enterprise. In our time material success has been easier to come by than happiness. However, success has not solved the main psychological problems of life, conflict and unhappiness. In fact, material success often leads to self-analysis, the question being, "Since I've got it all, why am I unhappy?"

There is nothing wrong with success, of course. It's the solution to such basic material problems as having enough food, clothes and shelter to survive. But what then? Despite our common misconception, success does not equal happiness because it cannot meet all our inner needs. What success can do is provide us with the necessary free time to explore, discover, and express our inner self. However, it's up to each of us to decide what constitutes enough freedom from material wants to allow us to act upon the central purpose of life, finding and expressing the happiness and creative power that resides in the Inner Self.

## The Parable of the Frustrated Engineer

To illustrate this point, let me share a story with you about someone who is successful but still searching for happiness.

Once a very brilliant, distinguished engineer, who had amassed a great fortune in the electronics industry, decided to seek out new areas of learning for his restless mind to conquer. After months of searching he decided to focus his prodigious mental powers on the goal of spiritual enlightenment. Naturally, he intended to apply his logical, academic skills and his business knowledge of efficient production to the task at hand. Accordingly, he called his travel agent and had him make plane reservations for Japan and arrange an audience with the abbott of a Zen Monastery. When the arrangements were confirmed, he calculated that it would only be a matter of a few hours before he found Enlightenment. After all, if academics and business had been easily conquered goals, it was logical that enlightenment, the most basic of simplicities, would present even fewer difficulties.

He arrived in Japan still excited and went directly

from the plane to the monastery. Thinking he would be there for one night only, he carried a simple overnight bag. After all, he had a golf date in Monterrey the day after next, and he was never late for an appointment.

Upon reaching the monastery he was met by a queer, little old man with a very wrinkled and weathered face and a foolish smile. In a courteous, but condescending tone, the engineer informed the old fellow that he had arrived as expected and that he had exactly two hours and forty minutes to become enlightened. His ancient guide babbled something incomprehensible in reply, pointed to a door off the hall, and left. The engineer, while slightly taken aback by this display of insensitivity, was not deterred in the slightest from his sense of mission. Opening the door, he found himself in a clean room with two pillows on the floor and nothing else. He sat down and waited for the abbott for over an hour, but there was no sign of his coming. By this time, the engineer was very nervous and upset. He stormed out of the room and, finding the first available monk, unleashed a stream of invective it would be quite impolite for me to repeat. When he finally got around to asking the monk why the abbott had not kept his appointment with one who had come so far to be instructed, the monk, who understood English, replied simply, "It happens. Come again tomorrow," and departed. Thus advised, the engineer was left alone, helpless in his rage. To his credit, he decided to give the abbott another chance. He would return the next day and teach these barbarians proper manners.

At the same time the following afternoon, he again reported to the monastery, where the queer, little man with the foolish grin greeted him and pointed to the same door as before. This time an hour and a half passed, and no one came to the room. By then, the engineer was so beside himself that he threw the pillows against the wall and stormed out of the room, slamming the door behind him. In the corridor he ran into the foolish, little man again, nearly knocking him over, but was so blinded by his rage, that he didn't even see him. Thankfully, he left the monastery without further incident and returned to his hotel. He had now to decide whether to return to California for his golf date or persist in waiting for the elusive abbott. After all, he never missed an appointment, and the abbott had rudely stood him up, not once, but twice. With his mind and body in a nervous exhaustion, he decided on an uncharacteristic course of action. He would cancel his golf date and remain to tell this abbott what he thought about his lack of courtesy and his totally unproductive methods of conducting a business. After all, how could anyone get enlightened when he couldn't even locate the teacher?

The next afternoon he returned to the monastery and was again greeted by the English-speaking monk, who also pointed to the same door and said, "The abbott will be right with you." Nevertheless, forty-five minutes went by without the abbott appearing. The engineer again vented his fury by picking up the pillows and throwing them against the wall. He was getting ready to leave the room when the door opened and the foolish, little old man entered, carrying a pot of tea and two cups, suggesting in simple sign language that the two pillows be put in the center of the room where the two of them could sit facing each other. Exerting tremendous self-control, the engineer did as directed. After all, he thought, tea and company were at least a beginning.

When they had seated themselves, the small, elderly man poured the engineer some tea. Since there was no bench on which to place the tea cups, our man held his cup while the old man poured. Unfortunately, the old man kept pouring until tea overflowed the engineers cup and soaked his trousers. The engineer, while politely trying to compensate for what was obviously the old man's failing vision, decided that this was too much. His pants wet, his leg burning, and his embarrassment extreme, he yelled, "Stop!" and called his host an old fool who didn't know his posterior from his elbow.

"Oh," said the old man, not in the least perturbed by this outburst, "I thought you would rather ask me why I poured so much tea."

The engineer, who had not expected the old man to speak English, was now more humiliated than before.

Finding himself in a state of nervous exhaustion and somewhat mentally unbalanced by all that had happened, all he could think to reply was, "Why *did* you pour so much tea?"

The old man replied, "You have come here seeking enlightenment, but you are too full of yourself. To find enlightenment, the mind must be empty and still. One must be flowing and spontaneous, not predictable and rigid as you are. Pouring this cup of tea to a state of overflowing symbolizes that you are overflowing with yourself. There is no empty space within you to discover the truth of your being, because your cup is too full of arrogance. You are not ready for the discipline that leads to enlightenment. After all, enlightenment is not a predictable event. You don't master it, it masters you but only after you have mastered yourself, by releasing your past and future hopes, your fears, and prejudices."

"Listen, old man," replied the engineer, stunned to the core by these remarks and not about to let this imposter get away with saying such things, "I have come several thousand miles at great expense to find enlightenment. I am very rich, very successful, and *very* well-informed. I have not come here to be talked down to by a senile old man. Now go get me the abbott!"

"But, my friend, I *am* the abbott, and if you can see beyond your arrogance you will realize that you have just received your first lesson. Now we will see what you are really made of. You must go back to America and empty your mind. Become open and humble. When you are ready, you may return."

At this point, the abbott rose and walked out of the room with great dignity. Since there was nothing left to say and only one thing left to do, the engineer boarded the plane for Monterrey to play golf and empty his mind.

## Intelligence and the External World

In our story, a good deal of emphasis is placed on the concept of emptying the mind. This contrasts markedly with our form of education which instills the idea in us that intelligence means filling our minds with knowledge about many things. Unfortunately, no matter how much we stuff ourselves with academic knowledge or surround ourselves with an opulent material environment, it never quite fulfills us. In gathering information about the external world and gorging ourselves on its riches, we run the danger of losing our connection with the Inner Self. No matter what we possess, we tend to remain restless, searching outwardly for peace while perpetuating our inner conflicts. We continue to gather things around us, thinking that "more and more" or "bigger and better" is the answer to life's riddle.

However, as the abbott in the story has shown us, happiness is a state of consciousness, not a function of how much we have. The central lesson of the story indicates that joy is the result of following a definite inner path firmly rooted in the discovery of our Real Self. Therefore the story suggests that happiness and fulfillment are a matter of inner or spiritual development and not solely under the jurisdiction of intellectual development and material reward, as we may have formerly supposed.

## What the Self Is

But what is this "Self" that contains such power to make us happy? It is a difficult question to answer because the Self remains something of a mystery, not because it wants to be, but because our language is not large enough to hold it. Language functions best by analyzing, identifying, and defining the component parts of things, while the Self embraces and is part of everything. While language attempts to define the visible, the Self represents what is invisible; a realm of consciousness beyond mind, emotion, and personality. Nevertheless, the Self, can and does express itself through these aspects of being.

The two major aspects of the Self are the Universal and the Individual. We define the Universal Self as God, while the Individual Self can be defined as that spark of the Divine within each of us. The purpose of the spiritual journey is to discover, reveal, and express the nature of our Individual Self, so that we can become one with the Universal Self, or God.

## The Beginning of the Spiritual Journey

The Spiritual journey begins, not by collecting more facts or objects, but as our story indicates, by emptying ourselves of our point of view, so that we can release our attachments to fear and conflict. To admit the new, we must pour out the old. For instance, if we want a glass of water, we don't use a glass that is already full of milk. Either we empty the glass of milk or get another container for the water.

The Self is very much like the glass of water. If we try to add the Self to a mind set that is already filled with prejudice or anger, the Self will be ignored or entirely distorted. However, if we allow the Self to flow into a consciousness that has been cleansed and prepared to receive it, the Self can transform us, making us into more aware, energized, creative, self-confident, happier people than before.

## The First Law of Consciousness

In this context, emptiness is the first law of consciousness. Imagine for a moment that each of us is similar in make-up to a circle, which has a center, a circumference and, between these two, a substantial amount of empty space. Likewise, each of us has an inner Self, which is our center, a circumference, or personality, and an area of empty space, which houses the mental-emotional matrix of our being.

Happiness and fulfillment occur when the creative power of the Inner Self is expressed through the medium of our personality.

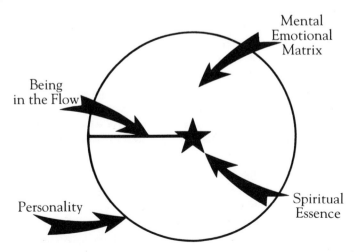

In the East, this process of linking personality to essence in order to express our inner spiritual creativity is known as "Being in the Flow." One result of being in the flow is that life becomes easier and more fulfilling than before because, by being in the flow, we attune ourselves to the power and creativity of the Universal Self. Because the engineer was dominated by his mental-emotional matrix he could only have an adversary relationship with both his Inner Self and the Universal Self. Being in the flow, on the other hand, allows us to produce a positive relationship with both aspects of the Self. As we learn to cooperate with the Inner Self, the Universal Self cooperates with us. Instead of working against ourselves and struggling through life, we can be in the flow and achieve success and fulfillment with much less effort than before.

## The Mental-Emotional Matrix

Before we can reach this state of powerful simplicity we must unravel the mass of complexity that binds most of us. The great stumbling block to being in the flow lies in the fact that the "empty" part of the circle, defined here as the mental-emotional matrix, is not empty but full of conflict. Since our mental-emotional matrix lies between our Essence and personality, it plays the very sensitive role of transmitting the inspiration of the Inner Self into valid, constructive forms of outward self-expression.

In this regard, the mental-emotional matrix is very much like a TV set that receives incoming signals and translates them into the picture on our screen. If we have good reception, we can tune into many channels and enjoy a wide selection of programming. Accordingly, when the mental-emotional matrix is clear and receptive, we, like the TV set, can tune into the many creative channels of the Inner Self, which we can then express for our own happiness or others' enjoyment.

However, if the TV antenna is disconnected, reception will be poor and the screen will be filled with static. Likewise, if our mental-emotional matrix is filled with conflict, negative thoughts and emotions, our inner receiving mechanism will also be disconnected so that we can no longer attune ourselves to the creative power of the Inner Self. When this occurs, we will find ourselves off balance and confused, unhappy and in conflict; consequently, we must struggle and work twice as hard to get anywhere at all.

Perhaps now you can begin to see how important the clarity and cleanliness of the mental-emotional matrix is if we are to fulfill ourselves. *Our Inner Self is always creative, whole and fulfilled, but our life experience will only be fulfilling if the mental-emotional matrix is clear and receptive so that we can experience and express the Inner Self.*

## The Problem of Separation

Unfortunately, as a culture, we tend to be out of tune with the Inner Self. More than that, many of us have never heard of this Self. One result of this cultural and educational problem is that we tend to think of each other as different and separate, without any real inner spiritual link between us. Modern man has become an alienated man. The question is how did the reality, or belief, in conflict and separation as the way "it is" gain such power? Why has the Self been discredited and ignored?

# Chapter Four

## Consensus and Conflict

*The day is not far distant when humanity will realize that biologically it is faced with a choice between suicide and adoration.*

Pierre Teilhard de Chardin

*With all being and all things we shall be as relatives.*

Sioux Indian precept

*Achieve results,*
*But not through violence.*
*Force is followed by loss of strength.*

Lao Tzu
*Tao-Te-Ching*

## Is Reality What We See?

We often think that reality is what we see. For instance, the chair in the dining room is discernible and solid, a structure having weight, mass and form. Since the chair is obviously there, it is therefore real. Yet a physicist would point out, that at the level of subatomic particles, the chair is, in fact, a swirling mass of billions of orbiting electrons, protons and neutrons. At the subatomic level, reality shifts from the physical solidity of the chair to a dance of atoms in motion. Which view, then, constitutes reality?

The answer to our problem is obvious. Both concepts of the chair are real: to the physicist, the chair is dynamic, changing and alive; to the carpenter, the chair is solid, stationary and inert. Reality, then, is a function of our point of view. There are as many realities as there are points of view. Since every person has his own point of view, there are billions of realities on this planet alone!

## How a Reality Consensus is Formed

If enough of us share similar ideas about the nature of reality, a mind set or reality consensus forms that allows us to define what things represent and how they function. Primitive cultures, for example, worshipped the sun and moon as gods. Modern man, on the other hand, having discovered some of nature's secrets, no longer thinks of these celestial bodies as gods, but as forces and energies that can be harnessed to fulfill his needs.

For primitive man, nature was all powerful and demanded obeisance. To modern man, nature is a field for study and conquest. Throughout recorded history, the relationship between man and nature has altered radically. Man no longer worships nature but conquers her.

Thus, we see that from a number of people sharing similar ideas about reality, a group consensus emerges, creating a psychological and emotional context or paradigm for describing reality. The prevailing consensus functions culturally to condition our way of living and thinking about the world. If, for instance, some members of our contemporary civilization were to assert that the sun is indeed a god and start a re-birth of sun worship, we would, from the context of our current consensus, perceive these people as somewhat foolish or neurotic. If, on the other hand, a scientist of our time were to appear in the world of primitive man, the scientist, in all probability, would either be viewed with the same mixture of awe and fear formerly reserved for the sun and moon, or seen as a bewitched and evil entity. *When* we were born and into what historical period we come has much to do with how we see the world.

*Where* we were born also has a great impact on how we view reality. In the traditional Western model of man, debate still rages over the thesis that man can gain voluntary control over his nervous system. In the East, voluntary control is an accepted fact of the Eastern reality consensus. In India, for example, there are many records of Yogis who have been buried alive for days at a time with little or no available supplies of oxygen. In some of these experiments, the Yogis were connected to sensitive scientific instruments that recorded their pulse, heart beat and brain activity. Although the instruments showed that the Yogis' vital signs were either very minimal or close to non-existent, they emerged from their ordeal fully alive. To the Western mind, feats of this nature are either miraculous or highly suspicious whereas they are acceptable possibilities in the Eastern paradigm. Obviously, our concepts of reality can differ from one continent to another.

Consequently, we can say that there is no such thing as a static, all pervasive reality consensus, for time, place and personal creativity all contribute to the different models of reality. Still the human need for security and stability amid the changing conditions of life creates a great historical dilemma: the need to go forward, while still holding onto the beliefs of the past, that may contradict, limit and even deny the ever increasing body of knowledge which has the potential to improve the quality of life. For every step forward, we seem to move one step backward.

## Limitation and Conflict in the Consensus

In working within the limits of a reality consensus, two major problems emerge. One is that the consensus limits our ability to discover what lies beyond the accepted description of reality. If we go beyond the prevailing consensus and discover new information, a new description, or paradigm must be created. In most cases, the majority is emotionally and psychlogically identified with the old consensus. Thus, new information is seen as a threat to all who believe in the old consensus, with the result that those who have moved beyond the previous description are often labeled heretics, fools, or madmen in order that the majority may more readily reject their claims and discoveries and preserve the old paradigm.

Historically, there have been many examples of this form of consensus conflict. Before Columbus discovered America, the prevailing consensus assumed that the world was flat, a belief that is supported to this present day by an organization in the American Southwest. Before Copernicus proved that the earth revolved around the sun, the prevailing consensus believed that the sun revolved around the earth. When Freud presented his theories about the subconscious mind, repressed sexuality, and the nature of psychosomatic illness, he was widely castigated by his peers and labeled a heretic and madman.

## The Nature of Belief

Consensus conflict, or the struggle to change our beliefs about the nature of reality, is obviously a highly charged process. Beliefs are ideas that we invest with emotional energy. Because we become emotional about our ideas, we identify with them. In fact, at the moment of emotional identification, we become our ideas. Our energy gives them life and vitality. This makes it difficult to be objective, rational and clear about the belief systems to which we subscribe. Instead of maintaining a dispassionate stance, we tend to become subjective, volatile and irrational about what we choose, or have been conditioned, to believe.

Because of their emotional content, beliefs, as differientiated from thoughts or ideas, are inherently violent. They are not as likely to be discussed as they are to become articles of contention. Rather than being ideas we can easily interchange, they are elements of faith which carry in them a desire for conviction, certainty and truth. Beliefs, then, tend to be absolutist in nature, and those who subscribe to them tend to become self-righteous and intolerant. To oppose them creates conflict and violence.

## The Evolutionary Impulse

Despite our sad history of conflict and violence, man's primal impulse is toward growth and evolution. History shows that the reality consensus does change. Nothing is permanent. The world is no longer flat. Conflict and violence are what man has passed through to achieve a greater vision of himself and his reality. Hopefully, as man evolves there will come a day when the human race will reach a level of maturity and clarity sufficient to cancel our propensity for violence. When that epoch arrives, man will have overcome his need to believe in something outside himself and come to live in the full light of his soul.

## Conditioning and Deprivation

The second major problem of working within the limits of a reality consensus is that the prevailing consensus conditions us to see the world and ourselves in certain specific ways. For instance, in our culture, we are taught to be analytical, cold and objective rather than warm, empathetic and loving. Conditioning implies that we accept external beliefs about the world and ourselves as real to the extent that we rarely question what we are taught to believe. Instead of searching for and discovering the truth within ourselves, we are told what is, or is not true. While this may seem to make life easier and more bearable at the very same time it deprives us of our right to explore our inner selves. We cannot know ourselves if we accept and believe, without first exploring. As the Greek philosophers admonished us over two thousand years ago, "Man, know thyself."

Obviously, there are two sides to every coin. If we accept that we should be analytical and objective while denying our potential for empathetic understanding and love, then we have limited ourselves to one side of that coin. Not only will we become imbalanced, but we will also be out of touch with our real Inner Selves, which can only be discovered when we express love. Thus, to approve the role models our consensus offers us is to accept ourselves as limited, alienated people, cut off from and deprived of our inner reservoir of creative power. If we are out of touch with our real source of creative power, we are more easily manipulated into what to buy, what to think, and how to live. That's good for the prevailing consensus and for those who enjoy political and corporate power. It's fine for Madison Avenue. How good is it for us?

## Contradiction and Expansion

Clearly then, we can say that a given reality consensus encounters contradictions that eventually will force it to expand. On the one hand, it creates stability; with the other, it denies growth. Historically, man has evolved and changed despite all odds; in a like manner the reality consensus also changes.

Man grows by changing his beliefs, by stepping out of limiting beliefs and into wider, more comprehending ones. Thus reality is not only a function of what we see but perhaps more importantly, a function of what we *believe* we see. And what we believe we see is based on what we will *allow* ourselves to see.

The less faith we have in ourselves, the more we will allow the conditioned belief system of the consensus to determine what we see. The more faith we have in ourselves, the less need have we of accepting all of the beliefs of the consensus and the greater will be our capacity to see what lies beyond. Interestingly enough, increased contact with the inner self will open our doors of perception to discoveries of our ever expanding universe. Where most models of the universe are generated and constructed from the level of the mental- emotional matrix and therefore contain the bias of the consensus, the true nature of reality can only be discovered in the deeper levels of the Self. Rapport with the Inner Self, then, is a powerful key to the discovery of the nature of Reality.

## The Role of Personal Creativity

Earlier we described two factors leading to consensus conflict, namely, the differences between times and places: Past vs. future, old vs. new, east vs. west. The third factor to which we alluded to but did not explain is the factor of the person, not alien to his consensus by virtue of time and place, but rather a product of it. Throughout history, we find individuals who were not dominated by the consensus but rather, were directed by their own wholeness and interior vision to give humanity the richness of their creativity and through their gifts, the possibility for positive change and cultural transformation. In the religious field, we find giants like Moses, Christ and Buddha. In the sciences, we find geniuses like Copernicus, Newton, Galileo, Einstein. In the field of invention we find, Alexander Graham Bell, Thomas Edison, Nicola Tesla. In the arts, we find prodigious talents like Michelangelo, DaVinci, Monet, Picasso. In politics, we know of great statesmen like Lincoln, Gandhi, Washington, Jefferson. In the new twentieth century field of psychology, we find Freud and Jung. Thus, at important phases in mankind's development, individuals of vision and talent have had the courage to stand up, step forward, and show us their dreams. Although we may have protested at the time this was taking place, their dreams, discoveries and related activities have changed the way we see the world and improved, to some extent, the conditions under which we live.

### Consensus Conflict: European vs. Native American

However, in our own past we have a very tragic, yet powerful, example of what happens when two contradictory reality consensuses clash. Conflict erupted when the European consensus encountered the Indian, or native American way of life. The European consensus is primarily left brain oriented while the native American consensus is mainly right brain oriented. A left vs. a right brain consensus is not a political battle between liberal and conservative elements of the same tradition, but a clash between an intellectual tradition and an intuitive one. Simply put, it is the clash of technology vs. spirituality. As the European consensus is primarily left brain oriented, it is based on orderly, linear thought processes which may readily be expressed in concrete, material values and activities. The European emphasis, therefore, is based on acquisition, property, power, technological and industrial development, and material success. In this mode of cultural organization, material science and technology have assumed much of the religious and spiritual power that was once the province of organized religion.

On the other hand, the native American consensus was and is based on right brain, spiritual values. The native American consensus was built on a belief in the oneness of mankind, the unity of man with nature and God, and the perception of a multidimensional spiritual reality. The native American consensus was not acquisitive and exploitive but preservative in essence. The native Americans were not universally interested in owning property because in their world view, it was not their property but the gift of the Spirit to them. In their view, they were the caretakers of the earth, not its owners. The native American culture, therefore, was more ecological than the European one which replaced it.

Moreover, the native American consensus as a whole was less interested in personal ambition than the European consensus and more focused on man's inner spiritual purpose and development. Thus the European tradition was more aggressively self-centered where the native American consensus was more receptive, compassionate and centered in the Inner Self. Where the European tended to see himself as the center of the universe and therefore woud abrogate as much power to himself as possible, the native American tended to see the Great Spirit as the center of the universe and would act in a more humble and sensitive manner toward creation. Where the European tended to base his morality, or guide for action, on the pragmatic need to either enhance or defend his power, the native American tended to base his morality on the attempt to act in accordance with the Great Spirit and perpetuate the harmony of life.

When the European cultural tradition arrived in America and began the push westward, gradually driving the Indian from his lands, destroying much of his population, and finally placing him on reservations with little natural resources, it was reasonably easy to justify the genocide of the native American nations. Because the Indians held different beliefs about life, lived according to different values than the Europeans, dressed differently and had different colored skins, it was both easy and necessary for the European to

view them as a primitive, backward, barbarous and dangerous people. According to this rationale, since the native
Americans were not like us, they were somewhat less than
fully human, and a threat to the expansion of our civilization.
Thus, the only appropriate solution was to protect our
consensus by destroying theirs. And this, of course, meant
destroying them.

## Cultural Imbalance and Tragedy

However, the destruction of the native American nations
was only part of the tragedy. The other part of the tragedy
was the missed opportunity for the two different consensuses to gain from the other; to interact, understand, learn,
and expand the limits of belief. The European consensus had
science, technology, and industrial development to offer,
while the native American consensus had spiritual vision,
intuitive knowledge and personal integration to complement
the prodigious European focus on material success. Since the
two diverging consensuses did not meet and integrate the
best of both realities, it was much like denying and
postponing the personal as well as cultural integration of the
right and left brain hemispheres. Thus, our culture is still at
odds between our intellectual, rational heritage on the one
hand and our intuitive feelings and impulses on the other.

## The Role of the Matrix in the Belief of Separation

As we said earlier, the European tradition was based on left
brain thinking. In terms of the circle analogy of Consciousness that we described in Chapter Three, we can say that left
brain thinking is dominated by the mental-emotional matrix.
As long as our beliefs about reality are generated from this
area of consciousness, we tend to see ourselves as separate
and distinct from everyone else.

From this perspective, there can be no perceivable
universal fabric that holds us together. One reason for this
failure to perceive the underlying unity of life is that
everyone has a slightly different mental-emotional matrix
and personality makeup. The other reason is that the Inner
Self is the domain of consciousness that holds our universal-
ity and oneness. If we are content to stop our exploration of

ourselves at the matrix, we will find neither our oneness with the human family nor our own personal fulfillment, for those states of consciousness lie beyond the parameters of the matrix and can be found only in the domain of the Inner Self.

If we are content to see ourselves as separate and different, it will not be long before we feel the need to compete with other people whom we also see as different and separate for a limited amount of jobs, shelter, food and other resources. Instead of sharing what is available, we compete for more than our fair share. In the process, we become threats to each other. As the process escalates, competition becomes conflict.

Consequently, whenever we create a reality consensus that is derived from, or based on, left brain thinking, it will tend to have elements of separation and conflict in it. These elements always have serious future consequences. They create fear, jealousy, hatred, war and destruction, not only threatening man's continued evolution but his very survival as well.

## Right Brain Values

The native American consensus, on the other hand, was dominated by right brain thinking. While the left brain is our conscious mind and therefore part of our ego and personality, the right brain is the door, or gateway, into the realm of the Self. From the level of the conscious mind and ego, we are all separate, but from the level of the Self, we are all part of the same universal consciousness. Therefore, a cultural consensus based on right brain thinking attempts to live in accordance with the values of inner harmony and external acceptance of all people. Instead of generating conflict, a right brain consensus attempts to create peace. Instead of creating hostility, a right brain consensus attempts to create social balance.

## The Need for Balance

Today we need the best of both worlds, of both realities. We need science and technology, but we need sanity, balance and spirituality just as much. Having one without the other places this planet in a position of great jeopardy.

Of course, it is both understandable and unfortunate that our European scientific and material heritage has denied the deeper spiritual and creative impulses within man. For one thing, the existence of Spirit is hard to prove with the scientific method. Yet Spirit exists. For another, the rise of western science grew out of a consensus in the Middle Ages that was based on darkness, irrationality and faith. The rise of material science is not only a reaction to that superstitious period but also has cast much light into that darkness. In so doing, science has seemingly replaced faith. Yet science without spirituality and faith, without a vision of the inner purpose of human kind, is as unbalanced as an irrational faith without science. The world demands balance, the union and integration of opposing forces, not their continual confrontation. Only with real balance can we really go forward.

If we work to rise above the conflict and separation of the conscious mind and avail ourselves of the creative power and wisdom of the Inner Self, we will not only integrate the right and the left hemispheres of the brain, but we will be able to create a reality based on sanity, responsibility, compassion *and* scientific development.

# Chapter Five

## The Path
## of Despair:
## Life on the
## Periphery

*"To be a true champion . . . one must explore the darkness, too."*
Eric Von Lustbader
*The Ninja*

*"The real lesson of the future is that it will be what we make it. Our actions—or inaction—will be decisive. We are now in command of our own evolution. The choices we make individually and collectively will provide the ultimate answer to our destiny."*
Maurice Strong, Former Director
Environmental Program of the
United Nations

*The sage seeks freedom from desire.*
*He does not collect precious things.*
*He learns not to hold onto ideas.*
*He brings men back to what they have lost.*
Lao Tzu
*Tao-Te-Ching*

*He who makes a show is not enlightened.*
*He who is self-righteous is not respected.*
*He who boasts achieves nothing.*
*He who brags will not endure.*
Lao Tzu
*Tao-Te-Ching*

## Security and the Inner Self

The Inner Self in each of us has the same potential for greatness. It is our source of creative power and energy, inspiration, intuition and enthusiasm. While each of us partakes of this same inner source our expression of these qualities will manifest in unique and diverse ways. From a shared center of unity our individuality develops in much the same way that different children of the same parents inherit the same family tradition, but, at the same time, develop into unique individuals.

If we mature spiritually and learn to express the Inner Self, we will experience happiness, fulfillment, clarity and security. When we give of our inner selves to others, we become stronger, clearer and more whole because we are expressing, and therefore *being*, more of our true selves. The sense of wholeness we attain when expressing the creative energies of the Inner Self may be the only real security we can find because when we experience our wholeness, we are free of fear and anxiety. In this regard, our sense of security is not as dependent upon how much we have or can acquire as it is on how much we can give and express of the Inner Self.

## Fragmentation and Integration

When we are in tune with the Inner Self, we are whole, and capable of expansion. When we are not in tune with the Inner Self, we are fragmented and incapable of real inner growth. Rather than expand, we contract. Instead of being open and clear, we become closed and filled with conflict.

Fragmentation is the process of a whole that is split into many parts. A fragment is a result of that process, a detached, isolated or incomplete part. Life on the periphery of consciousness is defined by an absence of inner wholeness and an abundance of inner fragmentation. Where wholeness creates balance, fragmentation leads to imbalance. Where wholeness produces clarity and vision, fragmentation leads to distortion. Where wholeness creates the sense of unity and mastery that we call being in the flow, fragmentation leads to struggle and hostility.

The opposite of fragmentation is integration. Integration is the function of a whole that does not break down but remains attuned to its inner center. Where fragmentation leads to conflict, integration results in creativity. Using the analogy of the circle to represent the function of consciousness, we can say that integration results when the Inner Self (the center) is transmitted through the mental-emotional matrix (the clear space) and expressed by the personality (the circumference). In this case the elements of consciousness, i.e. the matrix and the circumference, receive their directions from a common center, the Inner Self, which is the source of vision and creativity. When fragmentation is apparent the conflicting elements are in control. In such cases the most important element of consciousness, the Inner Self, is often completely ignored. When fragmentation occurs we are therefore dominated by external belief systems to the extent that our true vision and creativity cannot flow through us.

## The Search for Wholeness

Existing on the periphery of consciousness, in a state of fragmentation, we are forced to search for that "elusive something" that can make us whole again and provide us with the security that only our own wholeness can really bring. Often our attempts to overcome our fragmentation coincide with a desire to acquire status and material possessions. Usually, the more we acquire, the more attached we become to our possessions. Ironically, our attachment to possessions often increases our anxiety and tension to the point that the sense of security we expected to realize through them is completely destroyed. As a result, life on the periphery may further be defined as the search for wholeness through acquisition and attachment.

## The First Level of Fragmentation

The first level of fragmentation is defined as that in which the Self is completely separated from both the mental-emotional matrix and the personality. In this phase of fragmentation, the relationship between the mental-emotional matrix and the personality is strong and intact, while there is no relationship with the Inner Self at all. As we have said, we can only perceive the underlying unity of life when we are in tune with the Inner Self. When we are no longer in tune with the Inner Self, all we are capable of seeing are the differences and inequalities between us. When the vision of unity disappears, the spectre of conflict appears. Rather than helping each other and rising in consciousness as we would if our vision and integrity were intact, we instead attempt to rise in this world by overcoming and destroying each other. Winning at all costs supplants the innate urge of the Inner Self for growth, wisdom and service as the definition of success. The tragedy of life on the periphery is that by choosing to elevate the matrix and deny the Inner Self, we effectively cut ourselves off from our deepest sources of creativity, thereby denying our own potential for true greatness. The result is that we have created, and continue to recreate, a world that is imbalanced and populated in great measure by people that live in perpetual inner conflict with no conscious recollection of their true center.

## The Second Level of Fragmentation

As the competitive battle of life accelerates we move to the second level of dissolution: the internal fragmentation of the matrix itself. This stage is initiated when we begin to *react* to our life experience. Webster's Dictionary defines reaction as, 1. "an opposing action," 2. "a movement back to a former or less advanced condition," and 3. "action induced by resistance to another action."

For example, suppose you call me a bad name and I react by returning the favor. Then you react by calling me a worse name, and I, in turn, react by calling you the worst name I can think of. In the first case, I have opposed you. In the second case, you became even more primitive in your name-calling, which represents "a movement back to a less advanced condition." And in the third case, I have reacted in order to resist you or defend myself against your latest foul insult.

Thus, the more we react, the more we deny ourselves positive relationships with other people and distance ourselves from our creative source, the Inner Self.

As we continue to pursue a reactive course of behavior, acting aggressively and attacking others in order to defend ourselves, the more others will aggressively attack us.

Usually this will make us angry and more vehement in our own reactions. The more we allow anger and resentment to find a home within us, the more we attract the same kind of experiences that we had hoped to avoid. The roles and players may differ, but the themes will be the same. Our past will be repeated in our future. In fact, our past will often become our future.

## Reactive Behavior

A reactive course of behavior, then, only creates more and more conflict within the matrix. The more conflict within us, the more internal selves, or voices, we seem to have. Each aspect of our conflict has a life of its own and its own demands within our being.

All these inner voices and separate selves compete for attention in our minds and attempt to lead us into doing things their way. This creates both confusion and contradiction within the matrix. The more we react, the worse things get. The worse things get, the more internal selves we hear.

This cycle begins with the belief we hold that in this reality we are all separate from each other. Separation, then, creates conflict. Conflict, in turn, deepens our belief in separation. Separation begets conflict which begets more separation which begets more conflict. As the cycle continues, more and more fragmentation occurs at each turn of the wheel. As we become more fragmented, we tend to become more self-righteous and insecure. This tends to make us more rigid and unyielding which, in turn, creates more conflict. Finally, we become so angry and so powerless that we strike back at the world irrationally and often violently. As we can see, it is no accident that powerlessness and violence go together. We need only look at the current world situation. The threat of a nuclear holocaust, world-wide inflation, economic recessions and depressions, energy shortages, famine, water shortages, acid rain and pollution problems are simply the result of every nation, political faction and interest group competing for what it wants. Instead of seeing the whole, we focus on the fragment. Instead of acknowledging our interdependence and cooperating to create stability, we have chosen to compete, create conflict, and place the entire planet in danger. If we do not change course soon, we will end by destroying the environment, the human race and the planet.

## Contraction and Forgiveness

The process of fragmentation, is also a process of contraction. Whatever is incomplete or fragmented will repeat itself creating more incompletion or fragmentation. The more we allow this process to persist, the less dispassionate and the more hysterical our lives become. As we lose control of ourselves we forsake our capacity to act with power and clarity. This cycle, known in metaphysical terms as the law of Karma, will perpetuate itself until we learn to respond to conflict with love and understanding, thereby healing the separation, and resolving the incomplete pattern. The way we complete and, therefore, transcend the karmic cycle is through the process of forgiveness, which requires that we release our anger and resentment toward everyone involved in the situation, including ourselves. Forgiveness breaks up the conflict and "static" in the mental-emotional matrix allowing us to tune into the Inner Self and regain our creative power. By doing what is called "turning the other cheek" in the Bible, we free ourselves of the anger that both causes conflict and generates more conflict. Rather than closing ourselves off from both the world and the Inner Self, we remain in tune with the creative power of our inner source. Thus, the Christ was neither passive nor meek when he advised people to turn the other cheek. Rather, he was offering humanity the real road to power and freedom from conflict by union with the Inner Self.

When we lack this vision of our true nature, we are like a ship without a rudder, blown helplessly by any wind that stirs, with no compass to point us in the direction of our best interests. Without a vision of our true Self and what we need to do to maintain our connection with our essence, we become lost and fall easily and swiftly onto the periphery.

## Self Examination and Right Discipline

To decide if you are in tune with the Inner Self requires only an examination of your personal reality. Are there areas of continual conflict in your life? Do you participate in these conflicts by becoming angry and self-righteous? Do patterns tend to repeat? Or do you practice forgiveness by releasing your anger? Remember that unvoiced and sullen anger, resentment and repressed emotion perpetuate and increase conflict. When we withdraw by practicing forgiveness for all involved, including ourselves, we effectively withdraw our support from the conflict, causing it to gradually diminish and disappear.

Reactive behavior that causes and perpetuates conflict, or Karma, should not be indulged. Rather than reacting and losing control, we should learn self-discipline and gain control. Discipline means doing that which allows us to be yoked to, or in tune with, the Inner Self. Right discipline does not necessarily mean hardship, but joy: it does not imply suffering, but grace. Thus, right discipline allows us to express our creative power and act in the best interests of all concerned.

## The Role of Expectations

Reactive behavior often arises, innocently enough, with the expectations we have about the future. We create these expectations because of our need to escape the present, filled as it is with the conflict and anxiety of all that remains incomplete within us. Since our lives are not satisfying in the moment, we tend to look to the future for relief. Anytime we look away from ourselves and to the future, we create expectations. Our expectations signify that we are hoping things will turn out in our best interests; and hope implicitly means that we are dependent on the future for a solution to our problems. But since we created our own problems to begin with, only we, and not the future, can solve them. The task of self discipline is to tackle our problems now, in the present. If we choose not to exert self discipline our only alternative is to rely upon expectations and be dependent on a future that has not yet arrived. In doing so, we surrender our power to something that does not yet exist. By not expressing our creative power in the present moment, we are dooming ourselves to a failed future because it is what we do *now* that determines what will happen later. In this case, because we have chosen to hope rather than to act, all the future will bring us is a repetition of our current problems with a *greater* intensity.

## The Reactive Cycle

Unfortunately, when our expectations are not realized, we tend to implement our patterns of reactive behavior, with the belief that someone failed us, used us, or "did us in." This conviction allows us to feel victimized or persecuted. The next "logical" step downward into darkness and conflict is to blame or judge the person who has somehow offended us. After passing judgment, we can carry out the sentence and get even by hurting them as they hurt us. Sadly, all we get out of getting even is to feel self-righteous. And self-righteousness grows out of anger, producing tragic distortions of perception which alienate us from both our Inner Self and the people around us. Far from serving us, bitterness contributes to a heightened sense of isolation and insecurity.

If we persist in being stubbornly self-righteous and reactive we will continue the downward spiral of contraction which makes us even more rigid, insecure, powerless and prone to failure.

A diagram of the reactive cycle would look like this:

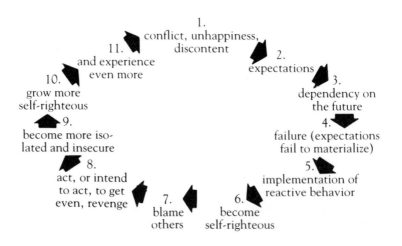

1. conflict, unhappiness, discontent
2. expectations
3. dependency on the future
4. failure (expectations fail to materialize)
5. implementation of reactive behavior
6. become self-righteous
7. blame others
8. act, or intend to act, to get even, revenge
9. become more isolated and insecure
10. grow more self-righteous
11. and experience even more

However, if we could admit our mistakes, we would not have to react. And if we didn't react, we would not become self-righteous. Sometimes, in saying we are wrong when we are clearly wrong, we regain our wholeness. And wholeness is real righteousness. The irony of the situation lies in the fact that sometimes by saying we're wrong, we really become right. But by insisting we are right when we are not and blaming others, we thereby lose our rightness and forsake our wholeness.

Life on the periphery, dominated as it is by the reactive cycle, implies that we can express through our personality only what is within our mental-emotional matrix. Since fulfillment does not occur unless we express the Inner Self through our personality, it follows that life on the periphery does not lead to happiness. Reactive behavior deepens our belief in separation, better known as the tragic human condition. We could just as easily call the reactive problem the drama of the darkness: Dramatic because we become more emotional, and less in touch with our true selves, and dark because the cycle represents the snuffing out of the life force of the Inner Self.

In the context of our circle analogy, the reactive cycle creates centripetal motion. The periphery spins inward on itself, darkening and polluting the inner space, and blocking the light of the Inner Self while at the same time contracting the energies of both the matrix and the personality. As the motion continues its inward process, it fragments us, decreasing the creative power we have at our disposal. The less access we have to this source of power, the more life turns inward and contracts.

## Contraction and Suffering

In this context contraction may be defined as the state where things work only through much effort and suffering. As the reactive cycle continues its constant downward flow, we can, in turn, define contraction as the state where nothing works even through intensive effort and suffering.

This should tell us something about suffering. From our perspective and contrary to what the church may tell us, suffering is an error, not a virtue. It simply means that we are not acting in our best interests because when we choose to suffer we are neither attuned to the Inner Self nor expressing its creativity. Suffering, then, is a warning light, or distress signal indicating that we need to change our course of action to one more attuned to the Inner Self. We can choose to martyr ourselves through suffering or become happy by correcting our errors. After all, emotional suffering is a voluntary activity. If we choose to suffer, we are only indulging and feeling sorry for ourselves. Since we have free will, the saner course is to choose to learn to express the Inner Self and experience joy.

## The Planetary Crisis

Unfortunately, the current world situation is dominated by the reactive cycle, filling the planet with powerlessness, violence, and suffering. The principle of contraction is increasing to the point where nothing works—even through intense effort and suffering. In light of the continuing world-wide fragmentation, it would be easy to internalize the despair and conclude that there is no hope for humanity.

However, this is exactly what we must not do. As we have indicated, suffering is caused by wrong actions based on distorted beliefs. In the previous chapter we showed how reality is based, not on what we see, but on what we *believe* we see. Starting with ourselves, we can change the belief that we are all separate by practicing forgiveness, releasing our anger, and opening our inner space to the light of the Inner Self. If enough of us decide to change our orientation from the separative tendencies of the matrix to the unifying ones of the Inner Self, we will not only discover personal happiness, but we will be able to build a safer, saner, more balanced world. Rather than rising at the expense of one another which only engenders hatred, we can rise together and make the world a safe and secure place where human beings, and the governments of nations that represent them, live not in the darkness of fear and reaction, but in the light of love and cooperation.

Life on the periphery of consciousness, dominating as it does the minds of most inhabitants of this planet, is only the first step in the evolution of consciousness. It is the phase of despair that leads to the time honored notion of the tragic human condition.

When we learn to find our way out of the reactive darkness by extricating ourselves from the illusions we have created, we will be ready to leave suffering behind and enter the second phase of development, the path of Self Discovery. Creativity, love and joy will then supplant fear, pain and conflict as the human condition.

It is our choice to make. The door of life stands open.

and conflicts are made more obvious. Finally, his lack of self-control is made fully apparent in his interview with the abbott, a traumatic situation specifically created by the monks, to reveal the engineer's weaknesses to himself. If he has the courage to honestly face himself, he will be permitted to return at a later date to learn how to master himself.

But for now he must return to America, and empty his mind of all false ideas about himself. This means that he must overcome his arrogance, impatience and sense of superiority as these are all veils which obscure his true self and prevent him from learning the lesson of self-control. These negative tendencies cause him to act in a fragmented and reactive manner. As he discovered during his stay at the monastery, he had little self-control. Instead, his behavior was determined by his negative qualities. He acted in the insensitive and arrogant fashion of a spoiled child. The monks then administered the necessary antidote of humiliation. Although the engineer probably did not realize it at the time, his humiliation was actually a great blessing. It provided him with the opportunity of facing himself as he was, without pretensions, but possessing real possibilities. While he misunderstood why this had happened to him, it was, nevertheless, an act of love and compassion for him on the part of the monks and the abbott.

## The Function of Love

Love, then, does not always mean being nice; rather, it means doing what is in the highest interests of all concerned. At times, love can be absolutely ruthless. After all, Christ threw the money changers out of the temple and called the Pharisees liars. These were not gentle acts, but they were demonstrations of Love. Christ, like the monks, created a situation of empathetic confrontation where those being confronted had their error revealed to them in no uncertain terms. While facing the truth about ourselves is not easy, it nevertheless represents an opportunity for constructive change, through which more of our Inner Self can find the light of day. Thus, the process of confrontation can offer the possibility of new levels of consciousness.

This does not mean, of course, that we can change ourselves only through confrontation, but that frequently it is a necessary teaching device. Because of the arrogance of the engineer and the Pharisees' false sense of superiority, confrontation was the method that would work most effectively. For instance, one doesn't tell an arrogant person how wonderful he is, as that only reinforces his haughtiness and prevents inner growth. The work of love is not always easy or graceful, nor does it make those who attempt to do it look saintly or benevolent.

Love does what is required. Real love is the capacity to meet the needs and requirements of the moment. Putting love into action takes courage, for we may have to risk our position, prestige, friendships and security to speak the truth if the moment demands it. This is the reason that great lives are not easy ones. Great lives demand the truth.

In the case of the engineer, he went to Japan with the definite expectation of becoming enlightened. As long as he had this hope, his experience at the monastery proved predictable. When his expectation failed to materialize he became self-righteous, blamed the monks and attempted to get even. This only increased his original conflict, making him even more rigid and insecure. The monks took advantage of his expectations to heighten and intensify his reactive pattern making him contract still further. By shocking him with his own negativity and lack of self control the monks opened the door through which he might change himself and seek the path of self-mastery, rather than expecting enlightenment to fall on his lap because he was "so wonderful."

St. Paul once said, "Pride goeth before a fall." Thus beware of expectations, for they only tend to stimulate the reactive cycle which, as it turns, will render us powerless and unhappy. By robbing us of our power, our expectations victimize us. Rather than change our behavior, we blame others.

Empathetic confrontation, as a teaching device, allows us to see ourselves as we truly are and thus to decide between our destiny or fate; for we must either walk the path of revelation or tread the murky way of reaction. If we see our reactive nature, we can respond by moving beyond conflict into unity. The opportunity that the monks gave the engineer was to see himself stripped of illusions, leaving him with the choice we all must face one day, as well.

## The Prodigal Son

The same issue of choice and resolution is wonderfully illustrated in the Parable of the Prodigal Son found in the Bible in the Book of Luke, Chapter 15, verses 11-32. To refresh your memory of the story, it is reprinted here.

*A certain man had two sons, and the younger of them said to his father, Father, give me the portion of goods that falleth to me. And he divided unto them his living. And not many days after the younger son gathered all together, and took his journey into a far country, and there wasted his substance in riotous living. And when he had spent all, there arose a mighty famine in that land; and he began to be in want. And he went and joined himself to a citizen of that country, and he sent him into his fields to feed swine. And he would fain have filled his belly with the husks that the swine did eat; and no man gave unto him. And when he came to himself, he said, How many hired servants of my father's have bread enough and to spare, and I perish with hunger! I will arise and go to my father and will say unto him, Father, I have sinned against heaven and before thee, and am no more worthy to be called thy son: make me as one of thy hired servants. And he arose and came to his father. But when he was yet a great way off, his father saw him and had compassion, and ran and fell on his neck and kissed him. And the son said unto him, Father, I have sinned against heaven and in thy sight, and am no more worthy to be called thy son. But the father said to his servants, Bring forth the best robe, and put it on him; and put a ring on his hand and shoes on his feet; and bring hither the fatted calf and kill it; and let us eat, and be merry. For this my son was dead and is alive again; he was lost and is found. And they began to be merry. Now his elder son was in the field: and as he came and drew nigh to the house, he heard the music and dancing. And he called one of the servants and asked what these things meant. And he said unto him, Thy brother is come; and thy father hath killed the fatted calf because he hath received him safe and sound. And he was angry and would not go in: therefore came his father out and entreated him. And he answering said to his father, Lo, these many years do I serve thee, neither transgressed I at any time thy commandment; yet thou never gavest me a kid that I might make merry with my friends. But as soon as this thy son was come, which hath devoured thy living with harlots, thou hast killed for him the fatted calf. And he said unto him, son, thee art ever with me, and all that I have is thine. It was met that we should make merry and be glad; for this thy brother was dead and is alive again; and was lost and is found.*

The most important characters in the parable are the father and the prodigal son. The father represents the Inner Self, always waiting and patient, eager to forgive, to express love and compassion. The prodigal son, on the other hand, symbolizes the personality dominated by the conflicting dreams and desires of the mental-emotional matrix. In his restlessness to break away from his father and fulfill his own ambitions the prodigal son epitomizes the first level of inner fragmentation, the separation between the Inner Self and the mental-emotional matrix. As the parable indicates, the son's ambitions lead to failure. It is, then, through the teaching device of suffering that the son eventually comes to his senses and returns to his father's house.

### The Prodigal and the Engineer

Certain parallels exist between the prodigal son in the parable and the engineer who traveled to the Zen Monastery. Both had experienced a certain degree of material abundance and had come to realize, in their individual ways, that there is more to life than material success. Each of them also was forced into the awareness of his separation from the Inner Self, although each one came to this realization through different situations. The engineer was placed in a contrived situation by the monks while the prodigal squandered his wealth. For both men the suffering became so acute they had no choice but to confront their own despair. At that point of conflict each of them faced a decision of whether to return to the Inner Self or follow the desires and ambitions of the separate self or personality.

We don't know what ultimately will happen in the case of the engineer. We only know that he was given the opportunity to choose and the option to return if he makes the right choice. Notice that, in this case, I have said the *opportunity to choose*, because as difficult as the situation seems to be for him, the opportunity to change his life and move from a fragmented state to an integrated one is his to make, provided that he has the courage to face himself, admit his faults, and overcome his reactive nature. In the process of inner growth, there are no free gifts. We get what we earn. In the prodigal's case, we know that he chose to return to his father's house, the Inner Self, where he was not only restored to his natural state of abundance but showered with gifts.

## Integration and Grace

As long as we are conscious of this opportunity for transformation we, too, have the same choice to make and the same possibilities for integration, or grace. This choice is possible because the Inner Self, like the father in the parable, is always waiting for us to return, so that it can energize us with wholeness, completion and love. Where we might see ourselves as full of pain and conflict in the lower court of the matrix, we can be freed from suffering in the higher court of the Inner Self.

## Free Will and the Inner Self

However, we will always have free will. The Inner Self will not enter our lives until we make the choice to open ourselves and re-establish this inner connection. That is why it is up to us. We must choose. The Inner Self has already chosen. It wants us to return and is waiting for us. But our Inner Self will never interfere until we are ready to accept it. We can choose fate, which will tie us to the far and sad country of the periphery, or we can choose to reach for our spiritual destiny and find our greatness.

## The Older Son's Failure

In the parable the older son hungers after his share of the inheritance as much as his younger brother, although in a much more subtle manner. Instead of being forthright with his father like the prodigal, he masks his greed and real ambition in a show of virtue; in the pretense of obeying his father and acting in accordance with his laws. This he does externally, but internally, he does not follow his father, the Inner Self, because he wants his father's possessions rather than real relationship with the Inner Self.

When the prodigal returns the older son grows angry because he feels his virtue has gone unrewarded, while his brother's transgressions are being celebrated by the entire household. As we know, the elder brother's outward display of virtue is the result of inner expectations. He thinks that if he is virtuous and does as he is told, he will be rewarded. When his brother is rewarded instead, the older son becomes reactive. Rather than join in the celebration, he accuses his father, and stalks out of the feast. As in the case of the engineer, this humiliating confrontation was precisely what the older son needed in order to see his negative traits, for it presented him with a crucial opportunity for growth. Again, the choice he made and the actual ending to his story is not known, but the impression seems to be that the older son turned his back on this opportunity and chose instead to wallow in despair and self-pity rather than open the door of destiny. Unfortunately, isn't this what most of us choose to do?

The Prodigal Son, on the other hand, now sees his relationship to the father with new eyes and new meaning. As a result of his experience on the periphery, he has undergone a shift in consciousness. This transformation has enabled him to drop the veils of illusion and false values from his eyes. He has achieved the spiritual maturity that comes when a prior path of pain and error is transcended. Because of his inner development he is restored to his abundant state.

## Knowledge and Inner Knowing

The relationship of the brothers to the father is indicative of another important lesson in discrimination: the differences that exist between outer knowledge and inner knowing. The older brother as a follower of external authority and convention is dependent on others. He lives, thinks and acts within the limits of the consensus. Through the process of risk and growth the younger brother, on the other hand, has moved beyond the narrowness of the consensus, and learned to think for himself. For the Prodigal, unlike his brother, the Inner Self is now alive with meaning and power, not merely the focal point of ritual and obeisance. Thus the Prodigal has nothing left to gain for he has found himself. Sadly, the older son has everything to gain, for he is still lost. Because he is dependent upon his expectations, the older son can be easily manipulated. Because he is in tune with the Inner Self the Prodigal cannot be conditioned and is afraid of life no longer. He now knows who he is.

As the older son represents the accumulation of traditional, external knowledge without an inner understanding of the nature of his own being, the Prodigal epitomizes the clarity of inner vision in which all truth is perceived. While the older son is caught in the web of ambition and desire, the Prodigal has discovered his inner purpose. He is now free to be himself, express his creativity, and experience fulfillment. Because the older son has chosen to remain in the separate state, he cannot enter into the celebration of the return. Instead he must remain on the outside, on the periphery of life.

## The Meaning of Sin

What we can further discover in the story of the Prodigal Son is the notion that sin is the choice to remain in separation and conflict. The Prodigal was saved, not because he confessed his sin but because he discovered his wholeness. Wholeness, then, not ritual confession, is the path to salvation. Seen in this light sin is neither absolute nor eternally damning, for we always have open to us the possibility of surrendering our conflict and discovering our unity. Like suffering, the notion of sin is a teaching device, intended not to rob us of power, but to force us to choose between conflict on the one hand and wholeness on the other.

We always have a certain amount of control over our lives because we always have free will. Nothing is precisely predetermined, because given the complexities of our situation, we always have choices to make. The quality of our choices will tend to determine the quality of our experience. If we see ourselves as victims, as the older son saw himself, we will not often make the right choice. What hurt the older son was not his father's actions, but his own expectations. His father wanted him to share in the celebration, because from the point of view of the Inner Self, both sons are equal. But the older son could not see this because he was not whole, or in tune with his essence. Thus he chose to react and experience suffering rather than joy. His decision was a bad one, not only because it caused him pain, but also because it obscured his own inner truth and diminished his creative power.

## Free Will: Willfulness vs. Willingness

In this case, the older son's exercise of free will was self-will. He acted in accordance with his own greed, desire and ambition. He acted only for himself, with no regard for his father and brother. Ironically, the person he hurt most was himself. Self-will, then, is reactive for it increases our sense of separation and deepens the hold our conflicts have over us.

In the case of the Prodigal Son, free will has finally matured into *willingness*. The Prodigal is willing to serve the Inner Self because he has found himself. Now that he is in touch with his source he can feel his unity with all of life. No longer will he act only upon his own ambition but now he will be motivated by the highest good of all concerned. "Not my will but thy will be done," becomes the credo of those who act upon the inner knowing of the Inner Self. When we act in this way we are willing to serve and help others grow as we have grown.

Because love makes us whole, and wholeness allows us to be free it follows that only the willingness to serve can lead us to freedom. Free will is only really free then, when it is expressed as willingness. When free will is expressed as willfullness, it only creates more confusion and suffering.

## Ambition and Purpose

In light of what has been said, we can see that there is an important distinction to be made between purpose and ambition. Ambition is the desire of the separate self to achieve a sense of security that was lost when the mental-emotional matrix separated from the Inner Self, as when the Prodigal left his father. Ambition, then, is a reaction to the fear of loss. In its primary form, it is an attempt to overcome the inner voices of doubt and despair that spring to life when we neglect the Inner Self, by achieving position, power, prestige, reputation, money, or any other tangible reality that we think will provide us with what we have lost. In the ambitious sense, we desire these forms of gratification because they tend to make us feel superior to most people or part of a special elite. Ambition, then, is a singular term. It works for what we want rather than for what is in the best interests of all concerned.

Purpose, on the other hand, works in an inclusive manner to help all those grow who are attracted to the love we radiate. As we regain our rapport with the Inner Self, we find the security that comes with being whole. As a result, we have little need of chasing separative ambitions. Rather than attempting to rise above other people, we are able to help others rise with us. By helping others, we help ourselves. Where ambition is a reaction to a sense of inner scarcity, purpose is the response to the knowledge of inner abundance. Where ambition competes, purpose cooperates. While ambition strives to be independent, purpose accepts our innate interdependence. Where ambition strives for wholeness, purpose is already whole. Where the morality of ambition tends toward greed, the morality of purpose is based in love: while purpose unifies us, ambition tends to separate us.

If we cut our hand, we are conscious of the pain throughout our body. The pain is not only felt in our hand, but affects the rest of our being. As the trillions of cells in our body constitute our person, so do the billions of people on the planet form the body of mankind. Whenever we create an imbalance in an area of the world, we add that imbalance to the rest of the world. What happens in one area ultimately affects all the world.

The problem of ambition has divided and disfigured the human family until mankind has reached a stage of critical illness. The function of inner purpose is to heal the body of mankind by helping all who so choose to discover the Inner Self and reclaim their wholeness.

## The Celebration of Return
The final phase of the parable of the prodigal son concerns

the celebration of the prodigal's return, symbolizing the union of the father and son, or the joining of the Inner Self to the mental-emotional matrix. The celebration represents the defeat of fragmentation and despair and the corresponding triumph of integration. In the integrated state, we are complete. The problems of the past are largely resolved and no longer hold us down. We are free to experience the present moment.

Contrary to the way it may seem the present is not part of a time cycle that progresses from the past through the present to the future. As soon as the present is experienced, it becomes the past. The present moment, therefore, is not so much a component of linear reality, as it is a psychological event, which can only be experienced when the three essential aspects of our being, the Inner Self, the mental-emotional matrix, and the personality are reunited. Without the presence of the Inner Self, there can be no true present moment, only the repetition of the past in our future. The presence of the Inner Self, then, is the key to all real change and transformation.

The more we express the creative power of the Inner Self and infuse the timeless aspects of our being into the world of time, the more we live in the present moment. This is the meaning of the celebration, as it symbolizes the integration of the three aspects of the Self. Thus, the feast celebrates the triumph of love over separation, the victory of unity over conflict, and the transformation of ambition into purpose.

## Mastery and Self Control

However, we cannot be enlightened, or filled with light, while negative tendencies still dominate our actions. That is why self-control is a preliminary step in the process of self-mastery. In order to learn self-control, we must work with the law of emptiness and resolve our incomplete experiences and negative tendencies within the mental-emotional matrix. Only then can we leave the path of despair and open the door to Self-Discovery.

The law of emptiness states that only when the matrix is empty of conflict can it be filled with inner truth. And secondly, that only when the matrix is empty can truth be expressed in our activities. Emptiness, then, is the necessary condition for truth to arise.

Once again, it is often easier to achieve success than it is to attain self-mastery. Yet success without inner truth has no real foundation and will not endure. In fact, success of itself often ends in tragedy. Tragedy, however, can provide the necessary impetus for real self examination and transformation, as illustrated in the cases of both the Prodigal and the engineeer.

As a teaching device, the parable of the Prodigal Son illustrates a critical point in the development of consciousness by describing the culmination of disillusionment and despair that usually occurs before we can begin phase two of our journey, the path of Self-Discovery. Before we open this new door, however, we must choose to leave the phase of darkness and despair behind. For we cannot enter the realm of abundance and fulfillment until we are committed to our destiny and working to resolve our past. The story of the Prodigal Son, then, is a story of movement and transition, from the periphery of consciousness to the path that leads us to our true center. Once we choose to grasp our destiny we are free to walk the path of greatness.

# Chapter Seven

## Unconditional Love
## and
## The Law of
## Expansion

*Because the sage always confronts difficulties,*
*He never experiences them.*

*Great fullness seems empty*
*Yet it cannot be exhausted.*

*Be really whole,*
*And all things will come to you.*
<br>Lao Tzu
<br>*Tao-Te-Ching*

**Love as a State of Being**

By now you have probably realized that we are not limiting
our definition of love to the feeling of affection we may have
for friends, family or lovers. Neither are we thinking of love
solely as an activity, like dancing or athletics, through which
we can express ourselves. Nor are we speaking of love as the
faithful adherence to a belief system which we regard as the
truth and in which we find security. While these categories
are real and legitimate forms of love, they share the common
problem of dependence upon an external form of stimulation for their existence and expression.

If we were to remove our family, friends, or lover, we
would lose our sense of connection and belonging. Deprived
of our traditional sources of affection we would soon grow
lonely and suffer accordingly. Or, if we were no longer able
to engage in the activities we love, we would tend to feel
frustrated and angry. Finally if our belief system were proved
to be untenable or misguided, our love of truth would be
endangered, and we would probably feel confused, insecure
and upset. Deprive us of reliance upon external sources of
love, and our sense of wholeness and well-being will
correspondingly diminish.

There is, however, another type of love that does not
depend on an external source of stimulation for its existence.
This category of love has an internal source and is determined by the quality of relationship we are able to develop
with the Inner Self. The more we express this Self, the more
we create the psychological present, or moment of integration. Our capacity to express real love reflects the degree to
which we are able to exist in the here and now. Love is what
we are, then, when we radiate the energy and life of the Inner
Self. Love can and does exist without the external stimulation of relationships, activity or belief, because love is an
inner state of *beingness*.

As we develop our relationship to the Inner Self, we will,
of course, continue to express love in the areas of relationship, activity and belief. In fact, with the evolution of our
wholeness, we will be able to express even more love through
these external forms because we will grow less attached to
having them provide us with a feeling of love. Rather than

being sources of love, these external forms will become outlets for the expression of the love that we already are. We won't have to look for love because we will be love.

## Love and Dependency

To the extent that our psychological and emotional attachments, or needs, decrease, our sense of freedom and wholeness increases. Because being love frees us from needing love, love as a state of being can free us from dependency on outside factors. We will then be freer to choose the most appropriate external forms through which to express love. We can now enjoy life more, because we are freed from the compulsion to pursue externally what we already are internally. Thus attunement to the Inner Self can improve the quality of all the forms that we choose to use to express love because what we choose will tend to resonate with the deepest and greatest aspects of the Inner Self. What we choose as a vehicle of expression will *extend* our sense of beingness.

## Unconditional and Conditional Forms of Love

The distinction between love as a state of being and love as a state of dependency on external forms of stimulation is the difference between unconditional love and conditional love. Conditional love is created by attachment, whereas unconditional love manifests through detachment. In the first case, we are trying to become whole; in the latter, we already are whole.

The fundamental problem of conditional love is that because we are incomplete, we are unable to live in the present. As we have said earlier, only when we create the present can we express our real Self and be love. Conditional love exists when we have neither experienced nor expressed the Inner Self. Conditional love, then, is the search for wholeness where unconditional love is the expression of wholeness.

When we are not whole, we usually seek love and approval through others. Our need for love generates expectations about what it will be like when we receive the love we need. Rather than sharing love, we demand it from others, returning our love, or approval only when our demands have been met. Love with strings attached is conditional love. Conditional love is aggressive, because it stems from a sense of inner scarcity, and alienation. Unconditional love is non-aggressive because it flows from inner abundance and self-acceptance. Conditional love spawns discord and disruption while unconditional love creates peace.

Conditional love penetrates no further into the mystery of consciousness than the matrix, where conflict and separation are powerful determining factors in creating our personal realities. If we are filled with conflict, suffering and need, our reality will reflect our inner liabilities. Getting others to love us, adopting a belief system, or immersing ourselves in activity are all ultimately unsuccessful strategies which extend the tyranny of inner conflict. We may be free of turmoil while fully involved in the various forms of external stimulation we have chosen, but when that involvement ends, the conflict reappears.

Unfortunately, conditional love tends to run on the hope that when we find love, we will be all right. As we discussed earlier, most forms of hope are doomed to failure because they orient us in the future and not in the present. The only solution for conflict is to come to terms with ourselves, confront our problems, and accept ourselves.

## Confrontation and Acceptance

Confrontation and acceptance are the solution to the problem of hope and its flight into the future because they not only focus us in the present but also allow the joy of the Inner Self to shine forth. Thus, where conflict bars the door to the domain of the Inner Self, self-acceptance opens it. Through acceptance of our conflicts, we can discover our wholeness and experience unconditional love.

As we experience and express the Inner Self, our conflicts begin to lose their hold and no longer control us. As we learn to accept ourselves with our own imperfections, we are able to accept others with theirs. Rather than expect and demand love from others, we will be able to give and share it, thus creating balance and equality in our relationships.

However, if we remain dominated by conflict and deeply involved in the pursuit of conditional love, we will be haunted by a feeling of separation from others, a feeling that has its source in our own lack of being love. By reaching beyond our conflict to the Inner Self, however, we discover that we are no longer lonely, but all one. We can then stand alone and share love with others, rather than being dominated by the need for outside fulfillment. Thus, what we are we can choose to share while what we are not we are forced to demand. The willingness to share versus the need to demand is then the essential distinction between unconditional and conditional forms of love, a distinction which makes all the difference in our capacity for happiness. The Law of Attraction states that like attracts like. If we are love, we attract love. If we have not yet become love, the attempt to find it often proves futile. On the one hand, unconditional love creates inner abundance which then allows us to attract positive life experiences. With the other, conditional love generates a sense of inner poverty which forces us to demand, and therefore alienate, what we cannot be, or attract.

## The Law of Expansion

What enables us to move off the path of despair to which conditional love continually subjects us is the willingness to exercise the law of emptiness and experience that sense of wholeness embodied in the Inner Self. However, in order to make our wholeness tangible and real, we must not only experience it, but also *express* it. The Law of Emptiness allows us to employ the tools of love, acceptance and forgiveness to go within the dark shadows of the matrix, heal our hidden conflicts, and experience the Inner Self. The next step must be to redirect our love energy from this inner focus to its external expression.

The principle of consciousness that allows us to move from the experience of the Inner Self to its expression is the Law of Expansion. According to this law, the more love we express, the more wholeness we possess. Since love is limitless, our wholeness is also limitless. Therefore, there is no end to our potential for creative power and happiness. The more we express our inner love and light, the happier and more fulfilled we become.

Seen in this light the key to expansion is the expression of unconditional love. Hence our capacity for the expression of love, (or lack of it) creates our reality. In this sense, we are responsible for what we experience. What starts with emptiness leads to expression and becomes expansion. This triad of activity creates fulfillment. What begins with conflict leads to reaction and separation, becoming the loss of the Self. This loss is the Great Illusion and gives rise to suffering.

In the three concepts of emptiness, expression and expansion lie the keys to not only overcome our personal problems and unhappiness but also to create a more harmonious and constructive planetary reality.

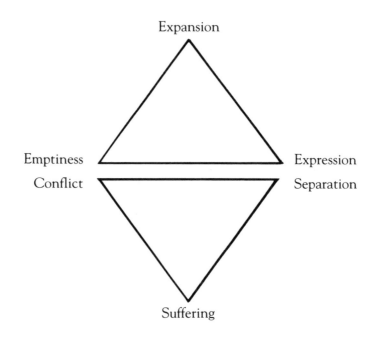

# Chapter Eight

## The Quest for Perfection and More Meaningful Endeavors

> *The sage never tries to store things up*
> *The more he does for others, the more he has*
> *The more he gives to others, the greater his abundance.*
>
> Lao Tzu
> *Tao-Te-Ching*

If we lack love, we often compensate by struggling to be perfect, which usually implies that we are trying to be something other than ourselves. In contrast, being love means that we have the grace and courage to accept who we are rather than trying to be something we are not. In this regard, acceptance creates harmony and integration, while the need for perfection generates conflict and destroys our sense of unity. The quest for perfection, then, does not enhance, but rather diminishes our real sense of Self.

The act of judging ourselves by an external standard of perfection, or comparing ourselves to what we are not deepens our dilemma by creating anguish and guilt in the matrix. As our sense of guilt escalates, we tend to repress the creativity and joy of the Inner Self.

## Self Repression

The act of self-repression prevents us from living in the present, and condemns us to the past-becomes-future syndrome of the reactive cycle. In this case, the more we fail in the pursuit of perfection the guiltier we feel and the harder we try to be perfect. This strategy forces us to replay our past attempts at perfection, in the future. This, in turn, makes us more rigid in our endeavor to achieve a state of unyielding, unchanging absolute perfection. We may not find absolute perfection, but we will become absolutely rigid. Trying to be perfect, then, is not a solution to the problem of living. Indeed, it only intensifies the problem.

## Perfection, Resistance and Change

Our physical reality, however, is a relative plane where we experience change at every step of the journey of life. Day turns to night, winter to spring, youth grows to old age. We may have been a "perfect" baby, or a "perfect" child in our parents' eyes but we have grown beyond these early stages and any attempt to hold onto our idealized and sentimental notions of perfection will only inhibit us from attaining greater growth and maturity. In this case, a willingness to be open and vulnerable, rather than the continued attempt to be perfect, is the real way to growth.

The assumption implicit in our notion of perfection is

that it is a state of being which stands outside of change: a condition that is at once absolute and irrevocable. However, the only absolute in this reality is change. The quest for perfection often isolates us from the very changes we need to experience in order to grow and develop. As a result, we can perceive the quest for perfection as the attempt to escape our need to grow as people by resisting the demands of change.

The need to be perfect, then, is a form of resistance to growth. What we resist runs us. What we accept frees us. The more we refuse to accept the challenge of growth because of our resistance to change and our need of perfection the more insecure and out of touch with the Inner Self we become. Instead of growing, we regress. This is the legacy of the struggle for perfection.

Since this is a relative plane, a plane of change and movement rather than a dimension of perfection and absolutes, we can most readily accommodate our need for growth and self-expression by first allowing ourselves to accept our experience, then correcting our actions and ourselves through what our experience teaches us. Rather than reacting unconsciously, and resisting our experience because we want to remain perfect, we should ask ourselves, "What is this experience teaching me? What can I learn?" If we search for the lesson, we will grow. If we react, the experience will be continually repeated in the future until we learn the lesson hidden within the experience. Viewed in this light, we can say that the reaction to growth and change creates resistance which then generates the repetition of experience. Thus, the need to be perfect not only fails in its goal of making us perfect, it also makes us less conscious, or unconscious, about the nature of our true Self.

## Self Acceptance is Perfection

Consequently, the only perfection available to us in this plane of relativity is self-acceptance. The more we accept ourselves, the more that which is perfect in us, the Inner Self, can be expressed. Where the need to be perfect focuses us in the future, the capacity to accept ourselves allows us to be in the present. Thus, acceptance, and not the quest for perfection, is an important key to the expression of our creative power. What we are able to accept, we can change. What we resist, changes and diminishes us.

## Love and Detachment

Love, then, is not involved in the quest for perfection, for love is not focused on the future, but centered in the moment. Since love is what we express when we create the present, *love is the ability to meet the needs and requirements of the moment while remaining in an integrated state.* The more love we have within, the greater our capacity to meet the challenges that arise without losing our consciousness of the present.

The quality that allows us to maintain our awareness in the present moment and radiate love is detachment. Detachment does not imply an aloof, cold, uncaring manner: rather, it simply means non-involvement in conflict. By remaining detached, we avoid reacting and preserve our relationship to the Inner Self.

On the other hand, if we were to allow ourselves to become involved in conflict, we would fall out of the moment because conflict deprives us of an integrated state of being. The more we grow involved or *attached* to conflict, the more emotional and powerless our lives become. In comparison, the more we remain, detached, or non-involved in conflict, the more clarity and creative power we have available to express. Seen in this light, we can say that attachment allows our problems to dominate us, while detachment empowers us so that we can overcome our problems. While attachment is a form of reactive behavior because it creates separation and causes suffering, detachment is responsible behavior because it creates unity and leads to joy.

If we are full of love, there is nothing to fear. We don't have to react. Rather, we can stay in the moment, in touch with our creative power and in control of our destiny. Thus, where self-acceptance allows us to *experience* the Inner Self and create the present, unconditional love and detachment allow us to *expand* our capacity to function in the moment. In essence then, detachment is the manifestation of unconditional love: its practice requires us to act responsibly rather than conducting ourselves in a reactive and defensive manner.

## Responsibility

In this context responsibility is the capacity to respond to life with love rather than reacting to experience with fear. Responsible action indicates that we are functioning from the synthesizing and unifying impulses of the Inner Self rather than from the separative tendencies of the matrix. At the level of Self we are all the same because we share the same spark of light and love, whether we are conscious of the inner flame or not. Interestingly enough we can act for the highest good of all when we clearly perceive our own best interests.

Responsibility and detachment, however, are not mastered overnight. We are on earth to learn how to be and express love. This takes time and requires learning many lessons. Each time we respond rather than react to a crisis in our lives, we learn an important lesson, earning the right to be more detached, in control of ourselves, centered in the moment.

As we experience our growing pains we should not get angry with ourselves if we are not always detached. None of us is perfect, remember! Rather than becoming angry with ourselves and creating guilt and conflict, we would do better to accept our imperfections. What we can accept, we are at one with and have power over. What we fear, however, has power over us.

Since the present is a state of wholistic integration with the Inner Self, its reality demands that we do not repress, but radiate our essence. When we radiate the love within us, our energy, power and awareness increases.

## Magnetism and Abundance

As our love energies expand we become steadily more magnetic. The more we give and share love with others, the more we attract what we need to both maintain and continue our growth. Love, then, through the power of attraction leads to abundance. In contrast, the peripheral consensus attempts to condition us to strive to accumulate and hoard material goods, having us believe that material success will lead to happiness. However, the law of love declares that if we wish to be happy, we must give to others that which we seek. Unfortunately, the peripheral focus on overcoming scarcity seldom attracts the security we seek. Only the law of love can lead us to both abundance and spiritual fulfillment.

The truth is, we don't always need a lot of possessions to experience abundance. In fact, the more we express our inner selves, the less material things we seem to need. Christ, Buddha, the prophets and saints had little more than the clothes on their backs, yet they were able to manifest what they needed, whenever they needed it. One thing, however, is certain: the less contact we have with our essence, the more material things we will need to compensate for our inner poverty.

Thus, we would do better to find ourselves before we seek material prosperity. We can then be successful on all levels of our expression. In addition, when we accept ourselves, we become less willful about pursuing separate desires and more willing to radiate love. The willing person is a free soul. The willful person is a prisoner of his desires.

How many times have you walked down a city street and noticed how sullen and negative most people seem? When we are focused in the separative tendencies of the matrix and ignore the Inner Self, we too will become sullen; for sullen means a soul locked in, unable to express its inner beauty.

## The Cycle of Responsible Expansion

If we allow ourselves to either remain, or become sullen and willful, our lives will be dominated by the reactive cycle that we described earlier in the book. The motion of this cycle is centripetal. On the other hand, responsible living allows us to function according to the opposite cycle of unconditional love, which may be illustrated in the following manner:

Emptying ourselves of conflict,
we find:

wholeness
and completion

leads to freedom and
expansion which creates more

living in the present
(no expectations)

find happiness
and fulfillment

create
abundance

express love

Where the reactive cycle produces centripetal motion, the cycle of responsibility generates centrifugal motion. Thus where the reactive cycle contracts our creative power, the cycle of responsibility expands it. The contraction of our creativity leads to suffering, while creative expansion leads to happiness.

In terms of relationships, the cycle of responsibility allows us to be whole and independent. From this stance we can move easily into interdependent relationships, creating harmony and balance in our interactions with others. The reactive cycle, however, leaves us incomplete and prone to dependent relationships. We may maintain a posture of independence but our relationships will be colored by negative drives and imbalanced tendencies. Rather than being able to love we will only be able to need. The reactive cycle dominates us through desire and expectation. The cycle of responsibility frees us through love.

One apparent lesson that comes to mind from the study of these opposing cycles is that the anger produced by reactive thinking cannot possibly help to change the world, while the love created through responsible action can help us to change ourselves. Responsibility is the way of love. If we are to master the prodigal tendencies within ourselves, we must let go of our reactive nature and accept our inborn capacity for responsible conduct. In this way, our innate creativity will find the light of day and blossom into beauty.

# Chapter Nine

## The Path
## to
## Enlightenment

> He who knows not, and knows not that he knows not,
> is a fool—shun him.
> He who knows not, and knows that he knows not,
> is a child—teach him.
> He who knows, and knows not that he knows,
> is asleep—wake him.
> But he who knows, and knows that he knows,
> is a wise man—follow him.
>> Proverb

> Love the world as your own self;
> Then you can truly care for all things.
>> Lao Tzu
>> Tao-Te-Ching

> To die but not to perish is to be eternally present.
>> Lao Tzu
>> Tao-Te-Ching

## Freedom and Responsibility

In the spiritual quest, enlightenment is the ultimate goal. For most of us, enlightenment implies both a great expansion of consciousness and a complete end to all conflict and suffering. As such, we tend to see our goal as a state of ultimate power, clarity, joy and love.

But there is another side to the enlightened condition that we rarely take into consideration, so hungry are we to escape our personal predicaments. What we often fail to perceive is that once we achieve an enlightened state, we are still faced with the suffering and darkness of those around us. In the enlightened condition, we realize that, while we each have separate bodies, different matrices, points of views and talents, at the level of the Inner Self, we are all the same. Because of our unity at this fundamental level, the enlightened person's responsibility is to help those who choose to listen overcome their suffering and their darkness.

Freedom, then, always confers responsibility. You can't have one without the other. The freer and more joyous we become, the more we can help others find the same freedom and joy. The beauty of responsibility is that by helping others discover what we know, we increase our own understanding of life.

The law of expansion teaches us that what is complete expands. Since the universe is a rather infinite reality, our consciousness, once complete, can expand to an almost infinite point. Enlightenment is certainly a state of completion, but even that exalted state is still subject to the law of expansion. Therefore, enlightenment is not an end, but a new beginning.

## The Two Realities

There are two basic realities. The first reality is the historical world. It is not infinite, but repetitive. This reality is dominated by cycles of separation, conflict and suffering. It is the world we live in. The second reality is ruled by love, joy and creativity. It is the dimension many of us aspire to reach. This is the world of enlightenment, the infinite reality.

We perpetuate the first, historical reality by believing in it "because that's the way it's always been." Once we identify with it, we increase its hold over us. Separation and suffering become the accepted way of life. As stated earlier, we tend to recreate our incomplete experience, both personally and collectively. Thus, the historical reality repeats itself, and through ages of repetition, comes to own us.

Within the parameters of the first, historical reality, we tend to think of freedom as doing what we want, when we want to do it. In this reality freedom is the fulfillment of desire. Unfortunately, the struggle to satiate desire leads to suffering.

In the context of the second reality, we can define freedom as the willingness to do God's will. We cannot do God's will, however, until we are complete, in tune with the Inner Self and loving. In this second reality, we create freedom through love and responsibility. The result of this divergent approach to reality is joy, clarity, understanding, and the privilege of access to more and more creative power. Thus, where the desire of the first, historical reality leads to entrapment, the love of the second reality leads to enlightenment. In fact, the only desire that works, and we define "works" here as that activity which leads to freedom, is the desire to be love and serve God by helping to uplift the consciousness of mankind.

## The Process of Becoming Enlightened

The challenge and responsibility of the enlightened individual is to help those who have accepted the historical reality experience the deeper aspects of their being and shift their reality from suffering to joy. The great paradox of the twentieth century is that as our capacity to destroy ourselves increases, so does our desire to explore our inner selves and fulfill our spiritual potential grow as well. Either we will destroy ourselves, or we will be reborn. Eventually, but unfortunately not immediately, the historical reality of conflict and suffering will be overcome as increasing numbers of people outgrow the way of despair and enter the path of discovery leading ultimately to enlightenment.

The enlightened state, however, does not occur overnight. It is a long, arduous process that, upon final arrival, seems sudden. In this regard it is like the rose bush which must be nourished then pruned cautiously, but unmercifully, for several seasons before the rose of great beauty "suddenly" blooms. The development of Christ is a perfect example of this process. Before he began his spiritual mission of teaching the law of love, he spent many years wandering through India, Persia, Egypt and Wales, learning and mastering the spiritual truths in these nations' highly metaphysical traditions. He did not start his public mission until he was thirty-two. The following year, his spiritual mission was completed with his crucifixion and resurrection. Nonetheless, long years of preparation were needed to produce such a brilliant, but brief flowering.

The example of Christ notwithstanding, we expect instant enlightenment in our current milieu. Since we can get instant potatoes and frozen dinners at the supermarket, we seem to think that we should find enlightenment, or salvation, just as easily. Unfortunately, nothing outside of ourselves can either save us or enlighten us. Enlightenment requires that we face ourselves, rather than rush to others to save us, or do it for us.

### Dangers of the Path

The most startling example of the dangers inherent in the expectation that someone else can do it for us, or to us, is the Guyana incident, in which Jim Jones ordered the mass suicide of hundreds of his followers. By giving both our power and responsibility to others, we become like leaves blowing in the wind, unable to do anything except follow the prevailing currents that sweep us up and away from ourselves.

If, instead, we choose the path to enlightenment, we must choose to own our creative power and exercise ultimate responsibility for our lives. Rather than being like a leaf blowing in the wind of the latest fad or political ideology, we must grow and develop like a tree with deep roots, possessing the strength to withstand any wind that threatens our commitment to love, service and truth. While weakness and fear will bow to the first wind that blows, truth and strength can stand firm in the face of the storm. As fear follows the drifting of the wind, truth can sail against it.

## The Need to Stand Alone

To be truly enlightened, we must, like the Christ, be able to stand alone, against all odds, opinions and powers, nourished by nothing but the Inner Self. Christ passed the test of standing alone not once, but several times. When he threw the money-changers out of the temple, opposed the Pharisees, waited for his captors in Gethsemane, and went to the Cross, he proved himself worthy of the pearl of great price. (And you thought enlightenment brought an end to all suffering!)

Before attaining enlightenment, we tend to view it as an exclusive condition, fit only for the spiritually elite or the lucky few. Upon achieving that consciousness, however, we realize that it is an inclusive state in which we find that we are neither special nor different, but rather part of the living fabric of God.

In the enlightened state, then, alone does not mean lonely, but all one. With the achievement of this apex of awareness, the personal and universal aspects of the Self are reunited. "I and my Father are one." (St. John 10:30) The difference between the enlightened condition and the unenlightened one is that the enlightened are awake to their true identity. The unenlightened still sleep.

## The Price of Enlightenment

Although enlightenment brings great joy, it often exacts a great price. We tend to think that when we become enlightened, all our problems are over, but actually all our problems may be just beginning. "To whom much is given, much is also demanded." Prior to reaching enlightenment, our main work involved self-discovery, self-expression and self-mastery. When we reach that goal, however, the focus of our work shifts from ourselves to the responsibility we have for others who seek our help. We must now help "them" achieve what we have won. The more detached we are able to remain, the more universal love can flow through us to inspire and illumine many other lives.

One of the many dangers on the way to enlightenment is the tendency to identify the universal love that can flow through us as our love, not Divine Love. Thus, while we may be loving, it is important to remember that it is God's love that does the work. If we are tempted to think that we are the source of power instead, our clarity and ability to channel God's love are vastly diminished. The resulting distortion of truth produces self-righteousness and moral, or theological absolutism.

## Dividing the World into Sinners and the Saved

Often those who feel they have been saved divide the world into the chosen and the damned. However, God's work is to bring all humanity out of the darkness of separation and suffering into the light of Love and Joy. Does dividing the world into sinners and the saved, or elite, bring us all together or throw us more apart? Christ said, "Before you take the mote out of your brother's eye, first taketh the mote out of your own." There are as many paths to the top of the mountain as there are people to climb it. Our ways may be different, but our goal is the same. Rather than judging others as sinners, we should develop our own capacity for love and detachment, laboring to correct our defects before we help others remedy theirs. (That is, provided, that they ask for our help. To offer assistance or shove our "kindness" down people's throats when it is not requested is inappropriate.)

Clearly, the truly enlightened person does not attempt to force his creed on others nor cure them of their "sinful" ways. Rather, the enlightened person sees the spiritual core, behind the imperfections and failings in other people, and works to bring out that core so it may blossom in the light of day.

Salvation can only occur when we recognize our Inner Self and express its creativity with understanding, love and delight. Thus, the enlightened person does not judge but loves. He sees what is hidden and does not judge what is obvious. In speaking to the hidden inner self and nourishing it with love, the enlightened person creates a climate where transformation is possible. However, if we think of the world in terms of the saved and the damned, we only create a reality where the notion of separation is invested with more energy and the possibility of real change and real salvation is ever more firmly precluded.

While we may believe we are acting appropriately if we pass judgment, we are, in fact, cutting ourselves off from the Inner Self. Every act of judgment separates the Inner Self from the outer self and disconnects our spirituality from our personality. The result of passing judgment is that we no longer see with the single eye of love, but with the complex eyes of self-righteousness and accusation. And the world, of course, is a very complex place.

This is not to say that we must suspend our critical faculties or stop making important decisions. It simply indicates that we should stop damning others and learn to listen with our hearts as well as with our minds. The more our hearts are open and illuminated with love, the less we will live in fear. As a result, we will be able to make individual decisions and enact social policies at a consistently higher level of clarity and truth. As we grow, both personally and collectively, as a people and a planet, the impact of decisions made at higher levels of clarity will not only help each of us but all of us.

## Overcoming Fear

Perhaps one of the greatest benefits of attaining an enlightened state is overcoming fear. To enlighten means to bring into the light. In the light, there is room only for love, compassion and joy. In darkness, however, there is a great deal of fear and anger. Hate will only exist if we are filled with inner darkness. Banish the darkness and the fear within, and all the energy used to hate becomes available for love and understanding. Feed the inner darkness, and the energy to hate not only will hurt others, it will consume us as well. Thus, where the universal light connects us to our inner source and helps us to express our essence, fear disconnects us from that source and prevents us from either knowing or expressing our real selves.

While fear and darkness attempt to teach us that we are limited beings, enlightenment teaches us the greater law, that we are beings of limitless potential. Christ turned water into wine, healed the sick and possessed, the blind and the lame. He walked upon the waters, silenced the storms of nature and from a few fish and loaves of bread, he manifested enough food to feed the multitudes. He raised the dead, finally raising himself from death. He displayed mastery over every phase of reality. This is true abundance.

Abundance, then, does not necessarily mean collecting great possessions and wealth around us. It means storing great wealth within us. At death, the rich person is forced to release that which he has accumulated on this plane, while the spiritual master takes his abundance, or consciousness, with him to the next dimension of life. Spiritual abundance means, then, the ability to manifest *what* you need *when* you need it. Christ owned nothing but the robe he wore, but he was richer than any man, for his consciousness was naught but light and love. He had fully conquered fear. Love, then, is the key to overcoming limitation and finding true abundance.

## Mastering Fear

On the path to enlightenment, we too will be required to face our fears and master them. In the beginning, this takes courage. Courage is the ability to persist in the right direction in the face of fear. Once we confront our fear, it will leave us. We will be the master in our own house. Fear will be the landlord no longer. Where there once was darkness, there will be light.

Often, in this book, we have spoken of consciousness as a circle with a center, empty space and a circumference. Every time we master a fear or a set of fears, we create a new line of access from the personality or periphery to the Inner Self. When we overcome fear, more of our inner light is freed from entrapment and flows outward into our life experience. This achievement not only empowers us, making us happier and more whole, but also affords us a glimpse of our real self and our true reality. Thus, each time we master a fear, we achieve a minor enlightenment. As the process of enlightenment develops, more of the Inner Self is freed for expression. Gradually, the Self expands from its point of origin in the center and fills the empty space of the mental-emotional matrix. When the Self has filled all of the space of the matrix, the process is complete, and we are enlightened. Everywhere we look outside us, we will also see the Inner Self.

After all, we can only see what we are. If we are living in darkness and fear, we will project our shadows onto others, accusing them of being what we ourselves are. If, on the other hand, we are whole and full of light, we will see that same light hidden in others. In the second reality of love and understanding, they too are just as we are. They simply do not yet know it. In the enlightened state, rather than project and divide, we will integrate and heal.

An illustration of the process of growth from darkness to light would look like this:

1. Consciousness: First Reality of Separation
    and Conflict

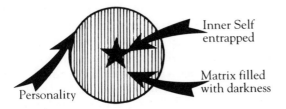

Inner Self
entrapped

Matrix filled
with darkness

Personality

2. Path of Discovery: Birth of Second Reality of
    Love and Understanding

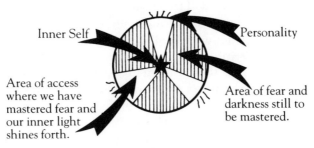

Inner Self

Personality

Area of access
where we have
mastered fear and
our inner light
shines forth.

Area of fear and
darkness still to
be mastered.

3. Enlightened Consciousness: Mastery of the
    Second Reality

The Self has
filled the matrix
with light!
We become a
radiant sun.

## Suffering and Uniqueness

One of the unfortunate ironies of life is that so many of us seek to be special, rather than work to become enlightened. From the enlightened standpoint, the only thing special about us, aside from our individual talents and forms of expression, is our attachment to conflict. Therefore, one of the things that make us unique is our individual forms of suffering! From the enlightened perspective, however, we are all children of the Universal Self or God, made from the same divine cloth. The only thing different or special about us, outside of the ways in which we express our individuality, is our chosen method of refuting our birthright. Each of us was given this life so that we might have the opportunity to wake up and discover our innate, ever-present connection to the Divine Source within. However, we can only discover that connection when we learn to love God as much as God loves us. While God's love for us allowed us to come into this life, only our love of God will allow us to fulfill this life.

God wants us to be happy, but God gave us all free will. We are free to choose to pursue either our own separate ambitions or answer the call of the greater purpose within us. The first choice will lead us to effort, conflict, suffering. The second will lead us through suffering to joy and mastery.

Eventually, we will all wake up and together choose the path of the Inner Self and the second reality of love, which alone can heal the problem of separation. After all, God can afford to be patient with us; he has all of eternity.

## On Top of the Mountain

While our paths to truth may differ, our understanding will be the same when we reach the top of the mountain. On the way to the summit, we will be faced with many tests and many challenges. If we rise to the occasion, these tests will strengthen us, clarify our direction and enhance our creative power. Each time a test is passed, more of our inner flame is revealed, more of our inner darkness, conquered. Each time we move forward into light, we will be greeted with less attachment and more love, with less resistance, and more flow. As we progress, courage will mature into faith, and effortlessness will replace struggle. Eventually, abundance will supplant lack and greed.

## The Ultimate Surrender

Finally, as we approach the end of the journey, that which is yet personal in us, which still speaks of attachment, fear and the need to be special, must die. Enlightenment is the ultimate surrender. The call of "thy will be done," at the entrance of the Path, must become at the end of the road, "I and my Father are one." At the summit of our journey, we must sacrifice the last grip of our ego and surrender to the impersonal and universal flame of love within. From this height of attainment, there will be no more limitations for our life will have matured from the attempt to practice love and live by truth, to being the very manifestation of these ideals.

If we were to place a sealed, but empty box in the sunshine, it would continue to contain its darkness. However, if we were to punch a hole in it, some light could enter. By gradually expanding the hole, we could allow still more light to penetrate. Finally, there would be no more darkness in the box. It would no longer be different from other boxes already exposed to the sun. Like everything else, it would be full of light.

We, too, are like the box. As we choose to enter the path of Self-Discovery, to grow and unfold, more light enters, and we become more open to, and in tune with, the universal flow. In the light of this flow, we, too, lose our need for uniqueness and become as one with the rest of the human family. Instead of being special, we become "holy," or full of light.

Our growth and our suffering, then, are in our hands. Shall we choose to reach for our destiny, or forsaking our potential, shall we remain chained to our fate? Will we be the masters of our lives or the prisoners of our own darkness? This is our ultimate choice.

Clearly, the path to enlightenment requires that we make the choice of engaging our potential; that we take the risk of seeking growth; that we choose to live in the greater knowledge, and second reality, of the Inner Self. This is not, at first, an easy path. Initially we must face the negativity within us and see what we would rather deny. We must see ourselves as we are, not as we imagine. We must learn to be vulnerable. At first our vulnerability will make us feel foolish and unbalanced, stumbling like a baby learning to walk. While this is often painful, it is powerful nevertheless, for it is the step of redirection. Eventually our vulnerability will grow into openness and strength. We will find that we have learned to walk. Our vulnerability will no longer make us vulnerable, but strong.

In having the courage to confront the shadows within us, we will see the truth beyond the curtain of darkness. In telling the truth about our darkness, we will see the light of our real selves. By facing the false self we fear, we will find the real Self we love.

## The Three Stages of Spiritual Growth

If we were to take a bucket of water that had a few inches of mud on the bottom, we would notice that the water above the mud was clear. But if we were to shake up the bucket, we would soon see that the water was no longer clear, but cloudy, even dirty. However, if we were to pour fresh water into the bucket, eventually all the dirty water and mud would be flushed from the bucket and only clean water would remain.

Most of us are like the bucket of water with a few inches of mud on the bottom. On the surface we may seem to be all right, but shake us up and all that we have refused to face within ourselves comes rising to the surface. It may be convenient and secure to attempt to keep the bucket from being disturbed, but it is also the path of least resistance and growth. If we can't reach beyond what is comfortable and occasionally assume a little risk, we cannot grow. Moreover, if we refuse to be "shaken up," so we can become clean and clear, the "mud," or darkness deep within our psyches will continually exert a negative, downward effect upon our lives.

This "bucket" analogy also illustrates the three fundamental phases of the development of human consciousness discussed in this book. These phases are, according to their progression, the paths of Despair, Discovery and Divinity.

The path of despair is life on the periphery. It resembles the bucket with mud on the bottom. On the surface things may seem to be clear, but on deeper levels, there is much darkness to face and overcome. At this early stage, our strategy, whether consciously chosen or not, is to hide our darkness, keeping it from ourselves. By doing so, however, we also obscure our light. In this state of limitation, we tend to react and repeat our experience, creating inertia rather than generating momentum.

In the phase of Discovery, we attempt to respond, rather than react, to experience. This allows us to correct our mistakes, learn our lessons and refine our self-expression. Rather than avoiding our darkness, we confront it. By doing so, we release our light. The water in the bucket becomes clarified. There now is little left to hold us down.

While the path of Despair is noted for its inclination to repetition, the path of Discovery is defined by its tendency toward refinement. As the path of Despair turns always in the same rut of separation, the path of Discovery turns on a spiral, moving ever closer to the real source of power, the Inner Self.

As we move on the spiral, we approach the final phase of development, Divinity. Here nothing remains in the bucket but clear water, for nothing can obscure the light and radiance of the Inner Self. This phase is characterized by the resolution of all inner conflict. The arduous alchemical process of transforming darkness into light is finally completed and the problem of life is resolved. The inner master appears: whole, complete and at peace. Nothing can shake us. Like Christ, we too can say on reaching the mountaintop, "I and my father are one."

The following table lists the different qualities of each phase in the development of human consciousness:

|  | Despair (Periphery) | Discovery | Divinity |
|---|---|---|---|
| Defined by: | Repetition | Refinement (transition) | Resolution and transcendence |
| Created by: | Conflict | Intuitive ideal of self-discovery | Unity |
| Operated by: | Reaction | Responsibility | Mastery |

| Motivating Force: | Desire | Love | Service to humanity |
|---|---|---|---|
| Resultant Force: | Contraction | Expansion | Infinity; completion |
| Emotional Response: | Fear and suffering | Happiness and understanding | Joy and freedom |
| Perception of the Inner Self: | Self-repressed | Self-released | Self-realized |

In this world, unfortunately, most of the human family still clings to the path of Despair. We can never discover our true greatness on this path. Because most people refuse to change, the level of conflict in this world increases. What was true a hundred years ago is true today. A house divided against itself cannot stand. To survive the crises and challenges of the present, we must choose to forsake the path of reaction and enter the path of responsibility and love. Everywhere the call goes out. Many are called and many chosen. But only the few have chosen to come forth. The fate of this world lies in our hands. Each day, the peril in the world grows greater. It is now time for each of us to change the reality of this planet by changing the reality within ourselves. The mountaintop is within us. So too is the path. All that is required is that we begin the Journey of Love to light and abundance. This is the only way we will find our real greatness as a people, and a planet.

# PART III

## Meditation

# Chapter Ten

## Meditation, Energy, and Awareness

*Meditation leads us to the inner work place. Meditation is a creative act that can lead us to the place where the pilot light of the flame of life burns at all times . . .*

Jack Schwarz
*The Path of Action*

## Forms of Meditation

Meditation is a form of exercise. Whereas physical exercise strengthens, tones, and improves the circulation of the body, meditation integrates the body's energy systems, relaxes the nervous system, synchronizes the hemispheres of the brain, and expands awareness. Like physical exercise, meditation requires consistent application to produce results. Meditating every day will produce better results than meditating once a week; just as jogging every day will produce better results than jogging infrequently.

As an iceberg has approximately seven-eighths of its mass submerged with only one-eighth of its reality above water, so too do our greater resources lie sleeping beneath the surface of our conscious mind. Where the conscious mind and its functions of analysis and sense perception may be more obvious to us, it, like the tip of the iceberg, constitutes only part of our potential. Meditation allows us to delve deeper and discover the potential of the Inner Self.

There are two basic forms of meditation. The first is passive meditation. In passive meditation, one repeats a mantram, a simple phrase, or follows one's breath. The function of passive meditation is to turn off the conscious mind, or the left brain, which functions on beta-level brain waves, and activate the right brain, which functions on alpha-level brain waves. Alpha rhythms are the frequency of meditation. When the left brain turns off and the right brain tunes in, the door to the Inner Self is open. As this door opens, we are gradually able to move from a limited, ordinary, timebound reality to one that is limitless and all pervasive. However, the transition into the greater spectrum of reality takes time and consistent practice. After all, we don't become olympic class athletes after a month's practice. Nor do we attain a realization of the Inner Self by meditating for just a few weeks.

The other basic form of meditation is active meditation. In active meditation, rather than attempt to shut down the left brain, we take advantage of the conscious mind's energy through the directed use of our imagination, to gain access to the Inner Self and the intuitive mind. One of the advantages of working with active, as opposed to passive meditation, is that in active meditation we can work more directly with the structure of our consciousness, which includes our energy fields and chakras.

## Consciousness and Energy

Whether we are aware of it or not, energy is continually flowing into us through the top of our heads. After it enters us, this energy is pumped first through the seven primary centers of consciousness known as chakras, then distributed to the physiological, emotional, psychological and spiritual systems of the body. The chakras not only fill the body with energy, but their emanations constitute what is referred to as the human energy field, or metaphysically defined as the human aura.

The aura, or the energy that radiates from our body, is an important aspect of consciousness. As our energy expands, we become more powerful, creative, and aware of the Inner Self. Thus, a main function of meditation is to increase the flow of energy through the seven centers of consciousness so that this increased energy flow can expand the aura. The principle at work in meditative practice is that *consciousness is a function of energy*. The less energy we have, the less potential for consciousness there is. The more energy we have, the more potential for consciousness we have. For instance, when you are tired, low or depressed, the world looks different than it does when you feel fresh, charged with energy, and confident in your ability. Moreover, the flow of this universal life force is as essential to our survival as air, water, and food, for it is the basis of our physiological ability to convert these essentials into fuel for the body.

## The Seven Centers of Consciousness

As energy is distributed through our being, it passes through and stimulates the seven chakras, which we have observed to be differnt levels or generators of consciousness. Let us examine them more closely. Chakra, which is a Sanskrit term, quite simply means a wheel. To the clairvoyant eye, the seven centers of consciousness resemble spinning wheels of light. The more energy we activate and distribute through the chakras, the more radiant and expansive they become, and the faster they spin. The faster they spin, the more awareness and creative power we have at our disposal. By activating and working with the chakras, we activate our inner potential. The chakras are not located in the physical body, but like the aura which surrounds it, the chakras are located just outside or in front of the physical body.

The seventh chakra, or center of consciousness, is the crown chakra. This is what artists rendered when they painted Christ, or other saints, with a golden nimbus above their heads. Esoterically, the function of this center is to make us aware and at one with the divine energy of the Inner Self. When we learn to function from this chakra, we will be able to say, like Christ before us, that, "I and my Father are one." Physiologically, the seventh chakra functions as the point where the universal life force enters us. Its corresponding organ in the physical body is the pineal gland. This chakra's primary color is a pale purple or lavender.

As the energy passes into and through the seventh chakra, it flows downward into the sixth chakra, located just in front of the center of the forehead. In the esoteric sense, the sixth chakra, or center of consciousness, is called the third eye. When we learn to work with it, we can see the "invisible" dimensions of reality, which, of course, include the aura and chakras themselves. The sixth chakra distributes the energy through the body by way of the remaining five chakras. The organ associated with the sixth chakra is the pituitary gland and its base color is indigo. A well developed sixth chakra, or third eye, also increases our intellectual and analytical functions.

The fifth chakra is located just in front of the throat. This is the center of creative self-expression. Is it no wonder that when we are angry, nervous, or afraid, we often have a "lump" in our throat? We cannot express ourselves creatively if we are upset or imbalanced because our energy flow is blocked, and the blocked flow manifests as the lump in our throat. The base color of the throat chakra is light blue. The organ in the body that corresponds to this chakra is the thyroid. Esoterically, the throat chakra is the center of clairaudience, or the ability to hear and receive instruction on the inner planes of life.

Next we come to the heart chakra. This is the center of both love and consciousness. The more we focus on discovering the love within us, the more our energies expand. Because consciousness is a function of energy and love is the fuel that increases our energy level, it follows that love is consciousness. The primary color of the heart chakra is gold. The organ in the body it corresponds to is the thymus gland. In most of us, this gland begins to recede when we reach thirteen or fourteen. At this age we are beginning to focus on what we want to become as we enter the competitive struggle for survival. As we turn our focus toward our physical existence, the organ connected with our higher consciousness, our spiritual survival, begins to atrophy. The thymus governs the body's immunity systems and as we turn our attention to survival, we not only turn our back on the development of our consciousness, but we also lower our resistance to disease. However, love not only raises our energy level, but also protects us from disease because when the heart center is filled with light, the thymus will not recede. Thus, by focusing on our capacity to love rather than focusing on our need to survive, we can continue our mental and spiritual development while at the same time increasing our capacity for physical survival.

As the energy proceeds on its descending flow, it enters the third center of consciousness, the solar plexus chakra. This chakra is located just in front of the solar plexus. Its base color is green. The organs or glands corresponding to the solar plexus center are the adrenals. This is the center of power and personal sensitivity or ego. If our consciousness is centered primarily in this chakra, we will be overly concerned or obsessed with our ability to have power over other people and the corresponding fear that others might take power from us. If too much energy is focused in this center, it is possible that we may develop ulcers. Fear about power and the need to protect and defend ourselves from conflict will literally eat away at us. On the other hand, this is also the center of growth. This is suggested by the fact that the base color of this chakra is green, the color of nature and growth. If we allow the energy of this chakra to flow upward to the heart after the energy has completed its downward flow, we can start the ascent into the dimensions of greater consciousness, joy and creativity that is *everyone's* spiritual birthright. In the Bible, it says, "Many are called, but few are chosen." A more correct interpretation would be, "Many are called, but few choose to come." The way of growth is open to us all. We need only choose it by focusing on love rather than fear.

As the energy continues its downward path, it enters the second center of consciousness, the spleen chakra. The base color of this chakra is pink, and the gland or organ connected to it is the spleen. This center is the reserve battery of the body. It is where we store energy. Since the cosmic or universal energy all around us is a form of love, it is not at all surprising that the reserve energy of the body would be pink, the color of love. When marathon runners hit the "wall" and receive their second wind, it is because the spleen chakra is kicking in and distributing energy to the body.

Finally, the energy arrives at the final center of consciousness, the first or root chakra. This chakra is positioned just in front of the reproductive organs. Its color is red. This chakra is the source of our sexual energy and our concerns for physical survival. When the energy reaches the root chakra, it should be redirected back up through the spinal column, released through the crown chakra and returned to its primal state of universal energy. The root chakra's role in the ascension of the energy flow is pivotal. This chakra should be thought of as a pilot light that ignites the energy and allows it to ascend up the spinal column, through the three lower chakras, into the centers of higher consciousness, the 4th, 5th, 6th, and 7th chakras.

## Survival, Security, and Power

All too often, however, our flame is out or too low and the energy does not rise but remains in the lower three chakras whose psychological issues are survival, security and power. If survival, security, and power are the main psychological issues of our experience, it follows that our reality will also be dominated by these problems. If our consciousness is dominated by conflict, then we will further legitimize and empower conflict by making it part of our social structure, our legal institutions, our government, and the interactions between governments. At every level of life there is and will be conflict. Why? Because we have not developed our creativity and are not in tune with the Inner Self. Rather than expanding and igniting our energy, we have allowed it to become dense. Now we are experiencing a worldwide energy crisis. Is this crisis not symbolic of the fact that we are also experiencing an internal energy crisis? Perhaps because we have misused our inner resources, we now face a crisis involving our external sources of energy. If we all would "fire" up our pilot lights and expand our energy into the higher centers of unity and understanding, creativity and clarity, then problems and conflicts created at a lower level of consciousness would be more easily and readily resolved at a higher state of consciousness. Keeping our consciousness focused on the lower centers to the exclusion of the higher centers only keeps the reactive cycle in active operation, increasing the likelihood of worldwide conflict.

For a moment, let us think of consciousness as a large glass. Imagine that we fill ten percent of the glass with coffee. The remaining ninety percent is empty space. If we try to look through the part of the glass that contains the coffee, we will see nothing but darkness. But if we decide to dilute the coffee by filling the rest of the glass with water, the coffee will be less concentrated. Moreover, we will be able to see through it more clearly. If we continue pouring water into the glass so that the glass overflows, eventually the coffee will be completely washed out of the glass and only water will remain. Under these conditions, we will be able to see more clearly than before.

In this analogy, the coffee represents what occurs when we do not "fire up" our energies at the root chakra and direct them into the higher centers of consciousness, the heart chakra and beyond. Only ten percent of our potential is used. In this state, we do not see reality clearly but through a glass, darkly. When our energy remains in the lower chakras, it becomes heavy and dense resulting in a reality which is dominated by issues of survival, sexuality, and power. This state of consciousness creates life on the periphery, dominated as it is by conflict and separation. If we keep our consciousness in the "coffee" state, we can neither recognize our own greater potential nor can we see other people clearly. Instead, we will see others in terms of our own separate sense of reality. Therefore, we will not really see them at all. Nor, unfortunately, can we really see ourselves.

Thus, we will often take the stance that you are either with me or against me: Conflict and separation. The world of the periphery is the world of alienation. In this world we are alienated from others as well as from ourselves. Unfortunately and tragically, it is what we have chosen to call the "real world."

## Transformation

When we add water to the coffee, we begin the process of reorientation and transformation. Adding water to the glass is like firing up the root chakra. It creates a state of expansion. What was dense is now free and flowing. Adding water symbolizes the process of self-discovery, of learning what is true and great within us. It represents the fact that we are more, much more, than what we thought we were. Our potential increases as our energies rise into higher centers of consciousness and we begin to see ourselves and others with eyes of love. We then realize that we each possess the same center and a similar potential. While we may all be in different stages of manifesting that potential, we are all journeying to the same mountain top. Our paths may be different, but our goal is the same. The more clarity we have, the more love we manifest. Clarity, then, is love.

As we continue to add water to the coffee, eventually all the coffee is washed away and only clear water remains. This represents the completion of the path when all personal prejudice and positions are washed away by the flow of love. At this stage, we are through becoming; the journey is over; the mountain top has been reached. We are now in a state of being, of fully knowing and living in the inner self. This is a state of fullness and calm, contentment and clarity, love and compassion. It is the state of a Buddha, the realization of a Christ. It is a state that is waiting for each of us. It is our destiny.

It is interesting to note that the Caduceus, symbol of the medical profession and healing, indicates a similar metaphysical truth. The caduceus is formed by a sword, two serpents, and a pair of eagle's wings. The serpents begin on either side of the sword and intertwine around it, crossing each other, in some versions three times, and in other versions four or five times. Above the third intersection of

the serpents in one version of the caduceus are the outstretched eagle's wings. The sword of the caduceus represents the spine. The three places where the serpents cross
symbolize the three lower chakras, and the outstretched
eagle's wings represent the heart chakra. The caduceus tells
us that the power of healing manifests when the energy rises
from the lower chakras and becomes centered in the heart.
Love, then, is the universal healing power.

The process of activating energy and raising it to the
higher centers of consciousness is greatly accelerated through
meditation. In addition, through meditation, we can tune
into and attract different qualities of higher awareness.
Earlier we said that each chakra has a different base color and
corresponds to a different bodily organ. They are as follows:

| Chakra | Color | Bodily Organ |
|---|---|---|
| Crown | Lavender | Pineal |
| Third eye | Indigo | Pituitary |
| Throat | Blue | Thyroid |
| Heart | Gold | Thymus |
| Solar Plexus | Green | Adrenals |
| Spleen | Pink | Spleen |
| Root | Red | Gonads |

Moreover, each color represents a different frequency of
energy as well as a different quality of consciousness. They
are as follows:

Red:      Physical energy and vitality.

Orange:   Intuition and emotional vitality.

Pink:     Personal love.

Yellow:   Intellect and conscious mind.

Green:    Healing for the physical body, growth,
          and physical balance.

Blue:     Clarity, peace, creative self-expression,
          and authority.

Gold:     Love and compassion, the foundation of
          consciousness.

Purple:   Spiritual power, inspiration, mastery.

Silver:   Detachment and higher sources of knowing.

Lavender:  Balance, harmony, integration of all aspects
           of being.

White:     All colors and higher qualities are contained
           in white. Thus, white is purity and Godliness.

In meditation, we can attract and incorporate into our awareness the different states of consciousness each color represents by visualizing a ball of that color above our head and then imagining a stream of that color flowing through ourselves and into our body, finally radiating into our auras. For instance, let us say that we are feeling confused and full of anxiety. Then we would visualize blue and imagine blue light flowing into us. Or, let us assume that for the moment, we feel stiff, rigid, uptight and critical. In this case, we would draw in pink, the color of love, so that we could integrate ourselves with our emotions and become more relaxed, gentle and loving. As a final example, let us imagine that we are writers or artists in need of inspiration. Then we would utilize the purple ray to attract inspiration to us.

The more we learn to work with the different colors, the more "water" we are adding to the "coffee state" of our consciousness. The colors we work with in meditation will help us to expand and explore the Inner Self. As we work with the different colors, we will develop reference points in our own minds for the change in consciousness that each color produces. The more we experience the colors and build reference points, the more of their energy and power we can attract, and the more creative and conscious we can become. It is interesting to note that as we become increasingly more familiar with the colors and are able to tune into more of their creative power, our auras will gradually become less bright and more pastel and subtle. This change in tone corresponds to our glass of coffee analogy. When water is added, the coffee becomes pale and pastel. When we raise our energies to higher levels, we begin to attract more and more of the white light of universal intelligence, or God, which blends with the different colors, rendering them more pastel in hue. Red becomes pink; animal vitality turns to love. Purple becomes lavender; inspiration becomes integration. Deep blue turns to sky blue; self-will turns to Thy will be done. Thus, the more we practice meditation, the more our consciousness is changed, purified and transformed. When we "fire up" our energies, we gradually move from a reality context of survival, sex, and power, which creates lack, separation, and conflict, to a reality consensus of love, creativity, and purity, which generates abundance, happiness, equality and peace.

In working with meditation, it is necessary to understand that the lower three chakras are just as important as the higher four chakras. They contain the energy that, when utilized and raised in a positive and appropriate manner, allows higher consciousness and knowledge of the Inner Self to manifest. The lower chakras must be utilized, not ignored or abused. Higher Consciousness means we are utilizing all of our consciousness, not part of it. The chakras are like the cylinders of a car engine. If one or more of them is not working, the engine will utilize its fuel poorly, the car will give a jerky ride, and acceleration will be poor and undependable. We cannot attain knowledge of the Inner Self if we ignore the lower chakras. Like a car engine with bad cylinders, it will be difficult to get anywhere.

The lower three chakras are our emotional centers. As my friend Jack Schwarz states, "emotion means energy in motion." Through meditation, we can learn to harness and control the energy in motion of the lower chakras and direct that energy to higher states of awareness, that are based not on reactive emotions, like anger or self-righteousness, but on responsive ones like love and acceptance. After all, we cannot build a fire without wood. The lower chakras provide the fuel for the fire of love and greater self-knowing. As we light our inner fires, we burn up the separation, conflict and karma within us, transmuting our consciousness into love and creative energy. This transmutation is the birth of the Inner Self. The Inner Self comes into being through the sacrifice of lower states of energy and corresponding lower states of consciousness for higher states of energy and higher states of consciousness. Thus, sacrifice does not entail death and destruction, but the transmutation of a lower energy state into a higher one. True sacrifice brings, not pain, but joy.

Meditation, then, is a practice of conscious death and renewal. We die to what is no longer needed or necessary and we awake to a new and joyous awareness of ourselves. Through dying on a lower plane, we discover that we are alive on a higher plane; through living, we prepare for death and expansion. Meditation teaches us the art that nothing true can ever be lost, only regained and known from a higher perspective.

# Chapter Eleven

## The Practice
## of
## Meditation

Meditation is many things. Fundamentally, it is the inner quest of self-discovery whose main goal is enlightenment; the merger of the Inner Self with the Universal Self. Before we reach that goal, however, meditation will enhance our development in many other ways. It will help us to raise our energy level, tap our intuition, solve problems, and become more conscious, compassionate, loving people.

In the previous chapter, we discussed some of the ways in which our energy system functions. The next step is to apply what we have learned and develop a meditative practice. The development of a daily practice is necessary because it is simply not enough to approach consciousness from an intellectual point of view. Without living what we learn, we cannot transform our reality. Meditation is an important tool because it connects us with our essence and shifts our awareness from the outer world of personality to the inner creative source of the Self.

At first, some of the meditations I have described in this chapter may seem long, but after you have read, digested and begun to work with them, you will find that they are quite simple, easy and effective to use. In some meditations, I have suggested a certain amount of time to be used in certain steps of the technique. This amount of time is suggested in the beginning as a guide to help you get used to the process. Later, you may wish to spend more time with some steps than others. Follow your own intuitive instincts. These techniques are not ends in themselves. If they were, the best you could achieve would be to become a spiritual technician. The techniques are meant to help you tap into, discover and express the Inner Self. Be creative with them. Let your own energy and intuition flow as you use them. Adjust them to meet your needs. After all, we don't want to be just technicians, but accomplished masters of the the Inner Self.

## First Meditation: Resolution (Law of Emptiness)

The aim of this first process is to empty the mental-emotional matrix of repressed material and incomplete issues from the past that still influence our lives, all of which involves relationship, either with ourselves or others. We can complete the past by releasing the experiences that caused us pain and by forgiving everyone, in our perception of events, who was a cause or party to that experience. There are no clear rules as to how often we should do this technique. Sometimes, once through the process is enough. More often, several times are needed, but never more than *twice* in one day. Release as much negativity as you can during the technique, but don't force it. Let it flow out of you easily and naturally. When it stops flowing, it is time to move to the next phase of the technique. Practice this technique with anyone with whom you still feel unresolved at present.

1.  Sit with your back straight.

2.  Take 4 slow, deep, complete breaths, breathing with the diaphragm and nose rather than with your lungs and mouth.

3.  Close your eyes and imagine that above your head is a white pyramid. (20 seconds)

4.  See the pyramid expanding until you are sitting comfortably inside it. (20 seconds)

5.  Then imagine a beam of white light flows down from the apex or top of the pyramid and enters you through the top of your head, filling your head and neck with white light. Allow the light to continue flowing into you, filling your chest and stomach, then spreading into your hips, down your legs and into your feet. Finally, let it flow along your shoulders, down your arms, and into your hands. When the light has completely filled your body, imagine it radiating beyond the limits of your body for three feet in all directions, so that you are now sitting inside a brilliant sphere of white light that extends for three feet all around you. (2 minutes)

6.  Now focus on a person with whom you are angry or a situation with someone that remains unresolved. Imagine this person sitting in front of you; then visualize a very bright and powerful, magnetic beam of white light emanating from your solar plexus and connecting you to the solar plexus of the person opposite you. (1 minute)

7.  Now visualize that this beam of white light acts either as a magnet or a vacuum cleaner and draws your negative feelings about this person out of you and into the light. Allow your feelings to be drawn out of you easily, naturally, and effortlessly. If you can feel emotions or see pictures associated with the person in question, just let yourself experience and release them, taking as much time as you need.

8.  When you have released as much negativity as you

think you can about this person for the time being, imagine that a knife cuts the connecting beam to this person, ending your negative emotional attachment for now. (30 seconds) If more negativity remains, you should repeat this technique with this person in mind at a later time.

9.  Now imagine a beam of gold light emanates from the center of your chest connecting itself to the same point of the person opposite you. (30 seconds)

10.  Send love to this person and forgive them for what you feel they did to you. Again, there is no time limit. (Do what feels right and natural.)

11.  Then send love and forgiveness to yourself.

12.  Visualize a knife also cuts this beam of golden light, thus severing your connection to this person. See this person turning from you and walking away down a country lane, passing through a series of gates which swing shut as he/she goes through it. Imagine that as this person continues down the path and away from you, they are walking into a tunnel of brilliant, white light. As they enter the tunnel, release them from your consciousness and thank them for the lesson they have taught you. (Your ability to forgive them and thank them is the measure of your progress.)

13.  Now imagine that gold light surrounds you, filling the white sphere you are sitting in with a golden hue.

14.  Take a deep breath, relax your focus, and when ready, open your eyes.

## Second Meditation: Integration

The second meditation will help you develop and increase both your energy level and your awareness by working with all your  chakras, or energy centers, to integrate the many dimensions of your being. This meditation should be practiced at least *once a day*. Whereas the first meditation helps you purify the inner space of the mental-emotional matrix,  this process enables you to fill that inner space with light. When this occurs, you will become a more radiant, magnetic and creative person.

1.  Sit in a straight-backed chair with your spine straight.

2. Close your eyes, take three deep breaths, and relax.

3. Visualize that there is a four-sided, white pyramid with a square base above your head. (30 seconds)

4. Expand the pyramid so that you are easily sitting inside it. (30 seconds to 1 minute)

5. Now imagine a beam of white light flowing down from the apex of the pyramid, entering you through the top of your head. Let the light fill your head and neck, then flow into your chest and stomach, through your hips, and down your legs into your feet. See the light flowing across your shoulders, down your arms and into your hands. Your whole body is now filled with white light. (1 to 2 minutes)

6. Visualize the light radiating beyond the limits of your physical body for three feet in all directions so that you are surrounded by a brilliant white sphere. (1 minute)

7. Now focus on the crown chakra located just above the top of your head. The crown chakra is shaped like a wheel, lying in a horizontal position just above the top of your head. (20 seconds) Imagine a beam of white light flows down from the top of the pyramid and enters the chakra, opening and filling it with energy, so that it becomes balanced. (30 to 40 seconds) As the crown chakra opens and expands, notice the colors within it (30 to 45 seconds), and attune yourself to its vibratory frequency. (30 seconds) Allow this vibration to penetrate your entire being. (30 seconds)

8. Now imagine that the beam of white light continues down through the remaining six chakras: the third eye chakra, throat chakra, heart chakra, solar plexus chakra, spleen chakra and root chakra. (See illustration.) These remaining chakras resemble wheels, which *vertically* align themselves to their corresponding locations in the physical body. Imagine this light opening and completely balancing each center. (30 to 45 seconds) Attune yourself to the vibratory quality and color of each chakra. (30 to 45 seconds) Then allow each frequency to fill your entire being. (30 seconds)

9. After you have finished with all of the chakras, imagine that the white light enters you at the base of the

spine. Focus the white light at the base of your spine and allow it to accumulate and build up. (30 to 45 seconds)

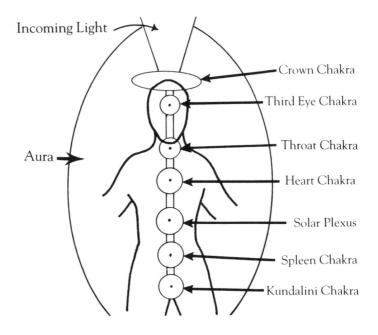

10. Release the light, allowing it to flow up your spine into your head, and then out through the top of your head.

11. As the light flows out your head, imagine it encircling you, so that you are now sitting in a great sphere of brilliant, white light surrounding you for five feet in all directions. (1 to 10 minutes)

12. After you have spent the amount of time you feel comfortable in the light, it is time to close the chakras. Starting at the crown chakra and moving down through each of the chakras in the same sequence we used to open them, visualize or imagine that the chakras, like flowers with many petals, close up, the petals enfolding towards the center of the chakras, "locking in" the light energy. (1 to 2 minutes)

13. Now take a deep breath, relax your focus at your own pace, and return to normal consciousness.

The reason we close the chakras at the end of the technique is that people who are unbalanced, negative and sick can unconsciously drain us of our energy, and we, in turn, can absorb their negative feelings. Since the purpose of meditation is to raise our energies, expand our awareness and make ourselves whole, it makes little sense to allow a situation in which exactly the opposite results might occur. Thus we close our chakras to protect our light. Moreover, the white light used in this meditation is the energy of the Universal Self or God, the highest and most powerful of all vibrations. It also functions to protect us from lower and negative energies because it is more powerful than all other energies.

As you practice this technique, you should find that all the chakras spin in the same direction. For most people, this direction would be clockwise if they were standing in front of themselves and looking at their bodies. As you practice this meditation, observe which way your chakras are spinning and make sure that all of them are moving in the *same* direction.

## Third Meditation: Expansion

Whereas the Integration Technique deals with expanding and balancing all the chakras, this third technique works with focusing energy and awareness in the heart chakra, the seat of consciousness. In the first and second meditations, you worked with the white light, the all inclusive light of Universal Consciousness, or God. In the third technique, you will be working with the gold light of understanding and compassion. Since understanding and compassion are two qualities of greater awareness, working with this light will help to incorporate and deepen these qualities in your being.

In the beginning it is advised to practice this technique once a day for three weeks. Thereafter, two or three times a week should be sufficient. Once again because we are all different, our needs may vary. The directions given here regarding how often these techniques should be practiced are all suggested in a general way. Feel free to experiment and adapt them to your needs. The only technique I suggest you work with on a consistent, daily basis is The Integration

Meditation, because it works with and balances *all* the chakras.

1. Sit in a straight-backed chair.

2. Close your eyes and take three deep breaths.

3. Imagine that above the top of your head there is a four-sided, golden pyramid. (30 seconds)

4. See the pyramid expanding in size, so that you are sitting comfortably inside it. (30 seconds)

5. Visualize a stream of golden energy pouring down from the apex of the pyramid and flowing into you through the top of your head. Imagine it filling your head and neck, then flowing into your chest and stomach, through your hips, down your legs into your feet, then across your shoulders, down your arms, and into your hands, so that your whole body is filled with gold light. (2 minutes)

6. Now imagine this golden energy radiating beyond your physical body in all directions for about three feet so that you are now sitting in the center of a brilliant sphere of golden light. (30 seconds)

7. Focus on the point at the center of your chest and there visualize a spinning disc of golden light with a diameter of twelve inches, about the size of a large plate. If you were looking at your mirror image, it would appear to be spinning very rapidly in a clock-wise direction. Focus on this spinning disc of light for 30 to 60 seconds.

8. Now shift your focus to the base of your spine. Imagine there is a small pilot flame, of the type found on a gas stove. As you focus on the flame, notice that the base of your spine feels warm and tingly. (45 to 60 seconds)

9. Imagine that as the pilot flame grows larger, warmer, and more intense, it begins to ascend your spinal column. When it reaches the level of your heart, visualize the flame flowing into the spinning disc of light in front of the center of your chest and becoming a brilliant cauldron of golden fire. (1 minute to 2 minutes)

10. If you have any problems or conflicts, notice where you feel them in your body and see them as a color. Now

imagine a gold beam of light flowing from the cauldron and attaching itself to the color that represents your problem. Like a magnet, it easily draws your problem into the cauldron, where the problem is consumed by the intensity of the golden fire. Then visualize another beam of gold light flowing from the cauldron and filling the space left in your body by your former problem. (Take as much time as you need to transform as many problems as you wish.)

11. Focus again on the immense energy in the cauldron. (30 seconds)

12. Imagine this energy vibrates through the following bodies in successive periods of 20 seconds each: your physical body, your emotional body, your mental body, and your spiritual body. You should not be concerned with the specific "location" of each body, as they are part of the subtle makeup of your energy fields. Simply allow your consciousness to create the suggested alignment, as it knows more than we generally assume.

13. Allow all aspects of your being to resonate together in this energy. (20 seconds)

14. Take a deep breath, relax your focus, and when ready, open your eyes and return to your present reality.

## Fourth Meditation: Manifestation

Einstein once said that imagination is the key to reality. This is just another way of saying that what we visualize in our minds can be physically manifested. Therefore, we should not always allow the external world to dictate our choices to us. Rather we should learn to choose what we feel is right for us and then create it. This technique will help us create what we want to have and experience.

There are two ways of creating. One way is through radiance, the other is through imagination and concentration. When we work with the principle of radiance, our assumption is that when we are fully ourselves, we will automatically attract what we need. If we are in tune with our inner abundance, that state will be reflected in our external reality. In order to make the principle of radiance work, we need to be loving, detached, centered and focused in the moment. If we are attached, reactive, dependent and have expectations, the principle of radiance will not work for us. According to the principle of radiance, we can have whatever we want, as long as we don't need it. Remember, the more in tune with ourselves we are, the less needs we will have.

The other method of manifesting our reality is to visualize what we want to have and then concentrate on it. To get what we want with this method, there are certain steps we must follow in the visualization process if we are to attract our goal. These are as follows:

1. Be certain you really want your goal and that it is in your best interest.

2. Visualize what you want to attract, as if you already had it.

3. See yourself having it in this present moment. (If you visualize having it in the future, it will always be in the future, and you will never have it.)

4. Make sure you are choosing a goal and not the process involved in achieving the goal. For instance, a woman I knew used this technique to try to get an addition put on her house. Instead of choosing the addition as her goal, she focused on winning a supermarket sweepstakes in order to finance the addition. She never got the addition. The lesson is, focus on the goal, not the process. If you focus on the goal, the process will take care of itself, often in simple, surprising and totally unexpected ways. But if you focus on the process, you will not only get lost in the process, you will actually disrupt the process necessary to achieve your goal. Your job is to focus on the goal! The subconscious will take your goal as a suggestion and create the best process for achieving that result. Only do the conscious mind's job. Don't attempt to do the subconscious' job too.

5. *Know* you have it.

Knowing what you want is a very important step. For instance, some years ago, I wanted a relationship with a certain type of woman. I visualized what I wanted and I got it. It was the worst thing that could have happened to me. It cost me a lot of money, a lot of time and a lot of pain. However, when I gave up wanting a relationship and forgot about it, I met the woman who was perfect for me. She is now my wife. If I had visualized what I thought was a perfect relationship, I could not have created anything to match what I have with Deborah. In my case, the principle of radiance works better than visualization and concentration. Sometimes it is better to let go, be yourself and have faith. After all, God knows what you need better than you do. The point is, if you wish to use the visualization method of creating your goal, be sure that what you want is in your highest and best interests.

According to different schools of thought, there are different focal points in the body for focusing your goals. These focal points are power points. One focal point is on the forehead, the third eye area. Another is at the back of the head, just above the neck. This is the region of the medulla oblongata, thought to be a point of direct access to the subconscious mind. The third power point is just in front of the center of the chest in the heart chakra. You may work with any of these points, but work with only one at a time until you achieve your goal. My particular preference is the heart chakra. Why? Because the universe is a manifestation of love and the heart chakra is the chakra that is the key to love and higher consciousness.

Whichever power point you choose to work with, the first steps in the process are the same. Take a piece of paper and write down your goal. Then write down three visual descriptions of you having your goal. For instance, if you wanted a certain type of car, you could see yourself driving it, washing it, showing it to a friend. Now that you have your goal in mind and your three images of having achieved that goal, we are ready to begin. This meditation should be done twice a day, in the morning and again in the evening.

1. Begin by doing steps 1-9 of meditation three on Expansion.

10. Then, in your own mind, say the following affirmation, "I am focusing all my power on achieving this goal . . ." (State what your goal is.)

11. Now that your heart chakra is open and filled with golden light, visualize or imagine that in the center of the chakra or either of the two alternative locations, there is a white screen, a smaller version of a movie screen. On this

screen, choose your first picture and focus on it for thirty seconds. Then choose your second picture and focus on it also for thirty seconds. Now choose your third picture and focus on it for thirty seconds as well. Now to reinforce your goal to the subconscious, choose your first picture again and focus on it for fifteen seconds. Then focus on your second and third pictures for fifteen seconds each as well.

12. *Feel* how wonderful and exciting it will be when you have achieved your goal. Emotion is a powerful tool that will reinforce the manifestation process. Always choose positive feelings. If you have trouble trying to create the feeling of what it will be like to achieve your goal, think of a time when you got what you wanted. Remember how happy and excited you were. Now focus that feeling on your present goal.

13. Now imagine a beam of golden light flowing out of your heart, carrying the images of your goal as far as your inner eye can follow. Then release the beam and the images of your goal commanding in your mind that they go directly to the Universal Mind of God.

If you have chosen to work with the other focal points of power, you may ignore this step.

14. Relax your focus, close your heart chakra if you worked with that power point, and return to normal consciousness.

## Fifth Meditation: Intuition and Guidance

In virtually all metaphysical and spiritual traditions, the concept of beings or entities from dimensions of reality beyond the physical world are considered legitimate and real. The following meditation will help you gain access to that part of yourself where it is possible to contact your own extra-dimensional intuitive sources. These inner sources can help us solve perplexing problems, offer information allowing us to make more appropriate decisions, and greatly expand our ability to know things, not through study, but through immediate comprehension or intuition.

Before beginning this meditation, you should have a pen and paper nearby. Write down some questions you would like to have answered. Initially, it is better to choose questions to which few emotional charges are attached. The more emotion you invest in your question, the less likely you are to get a high-quality reply. Conversely, the less emotional the questions, the more likely you are to receive an appropriate answer.

When it comes time to ask your questions, open your eyes and write down whatever answers come to mind. Do not evaluate or judge your thoughts, as this tends to interfere with the flow of information. Answers can be evaluated later. When you are finished with one question, go on to the next one. The more you practice the technique, the better at it you will become.

This technique again uses steps 1-9 of meditation three.

10. Repeat in your mind the following affirmation: "I surround and protect myself with the Universal Light of Consciousness. Only those energies which resonate with my Inner Self can enter my presence. I am invulnerable to all but that which is in my highest interest. In the Light of the Universal Mind of God, this is so."

11. Imagine that you are standing in front of yourself, looking at your physical body. (20-30 seconds)

12. Imagine that you are now walking into your heart chakra. Visualize yourself on a path in a forest, noticing its various sights and scents. (30 seconds)

13. As you walk along the path, notice it opens on a clearing, at the center of which is a small chapel or schoolhouse. Approach the building and enter it. (30 seconds)

14. As you enter the building, notice that there is a comfortable chair waiting for you in the center of an inviting and peaceful room. When you reach the chair, sit down. (30 seconds)

15. Imagine a teacher, spiritual guide, or someone with whom you are comfortable, appearing directly before you. (30 seconds)

16. See a beam of gold light flowing from the center of your teacher or guide's chest to the center of your chest. Imagine the gold light of love and understanding flowing to you through this connection. (45 seconds)

17. Imagine that your teacher comes closer to you and touches you on the top of your head, opening and balancing your crown chakra with white light. (30 seconds)

18. Ask your first question (45-60 seconds) and write down your answer.

19. Imagine that your teacher now touches you on the third eye chakra, filling this chakra with white light, balancing it and expanding it. (30 seconds)

20. Ask your second question (45-60 seconds) and write down your answer.

21. Imagine that your teacher or guide touches you on the throat chakra, filling this chakra with white light, balancing and expanding it. (30 seconds)

22. Ask your remaining questions (as much time as is necessary) and write down your answers.

23. Thank your teacher or guide for coming. Imagine that your teacher moves away from you. Stand up and leave the room. Walk back outside into the clearing, and then down the path to the edge of the forest. Step out of your heart chakra, and as you do, gently allow yourself to come back to normal consciousness. Take a deep breath, relax your focus, and when ready, open your eyes.

## Sixth Meditation: Night Time Review

All too often we go to bed with the cares and conflicts of the day unresolved and festering within ourselves. Conflict and anxiety interfere with the subconscious mind's ability to repair and energize the physical body, so that we often awake the following morning as tired as we were the night before. This meditation will help release conflict and accumulated stress from the subconscious so that you will be able to get a good night's sleep. The first half of this technique is best done sitting up in bed while the second half may be done lying down on your back.

Part One: Sitting

1. Breathe deeply three times and visualize a cloud of sky-blue energy in front of your face. On the in-breath,

breathe in the blue light. On the out-breath, breathe out your tensions and tiredness.

2.  Visualize what you want to attract, as if you already have it.

3.  See it expand in size so that you are sitting comfortably inside it. (15-30 seconds)

4.  Now imagine a stream of light blue light flowing downward and entering your body through the top of your head. Visualize the light filling your head and neck, your chest and stomach, then your hips, legs and feet. Finally , the light flows across your shoulders, down your arms and into your hands. Now that your body is completely full of light blue energy, visualize the light extending from your body for three feet in all directions, surrounding you in a brilliant blue sphere of light. (1-3 minutes)

5.  Visualize a white screen in front of you. On this screen visualize recent events and play back the "day's filming" from morning to evening. If there were any particularly difficult or painful moments during the day, stop the film when you reach them and visualize those frames being filled with white light until the images dissolve. Take as much time as you need to review the events of the day.

6.  Now, if you wish, you may lie down on your back for the second part of this process.

Part Two: Lying Down

7.  Begin by tensing and relaxing different parts of the body. Tense the muscles of the feet and legs. Hold that tension. (5 seconds) Tense the muscles of the hips and buttocks. Hold that tension. (5 seconds) Tense the muscles of the stomach and chest. Hold that tension. (5 seconds) Make two fists. Tense the muscles of the arms and hands. Hold that tension. (5 seconds) Tense the muscles of the neck and head. Hold that tension. (5 seconds)

8.  Take a deep breath and relax.

9.  Now imagine that you are on an elevator on the top floor of a skyscraper and about to descend into deeper and deeper levels of progressive relaxation.

10. Begin counting down from 100 to 0, allowing yourself to progress to a deeper state of relaxation the farther down you go. Move from 100 down to 99, down to 98, 97,
down to 94, 93, 92, down to 90
down to 80
down to 70
down to 60
deeper down to 50
still deeper down to 40
down to 30
down to 20
down deeper even to 10
down to the deepest level of relaxation 0

11. At this level, the subconscious is in a state of deep rapport with the conscious mind. Whatever we suggest to the subconscious mind will be taken as direction and eventually manifested in our experience. Now suggest in your own mind that you fall asleep easily and quickly, waking in the morning feeling refreshed, energized and eager for the day's activities.

12. Take a deep breath and fall easily asleep.

**Seventh Meditation: Reorientation**

In order to keep yourself focused on living in the moment and expressing love throughout the practical and mundane necessities of the day, do the following exercise:

Visualize a ball of gold light in your heart. Imagine this gold light radiating throughout your body. Imagine the gold light encompassing everyone in your immediate environment.

This exercise takes but a moment and can be done with your eyes open. Do it many times a day. The results you get from it may surprise you.

If you'd rather not take the time to commit these meditations to memory, they have been made especially available for your use on a special tape cassette. To order one, just write us at the address given at the end of the book.

# PART IV

## Appendix

me apprehensive because I thought she might still be in bad shape, and the walk from her room to the door might be more than she could handle. Fortunately, I need not have worried. When she came to the door, she stood there beaming. She had been in the middle of housecleaning and wanted to finish sweeping the kitchen floor before she came to the door. I could see she was eager to get back to work, so I stayed for only a moment. She said that for the first time in ages she had been able to get a full night's sleep. Her bruises weren't bothering her anymore. She didn't need people to help her walk. She was obviously full of energy and feeling very much better. Her skin was no longer pale, but had a reddish-golden tone to it, as if she had been in the sun for hours. The next day, the doctor removed the packing from her nose. Not bad for a woman who was in bad shape only fifteen hours earlier.

In the spring of 1980, my fiancee, Deborah, was in London, staying with an English family made up of Paul and Oss Brown and their daughter, Johanna. After completing a workshop tour through Boston, New York and Philadelphia, I went on to London to join Deborah for a two-week visit. Paul's mother owned a house around the corner from his which was unoccupied at the time. He graciously arranged for us to stay there while I was in London. A couple of days after my arrival, Paul and Oss invited us for dinner. Paul is a hard worker who starts his days at 5:30 a.m. and is exhausted by 9:30 in the evening. After supper, he was very weary and had a headache. I asked him if he would like some energy. He said, "Sure," not knowing what I had in mind, but trying to be polite and accommodate me. I didn't do anything visibly but continued to remain where I was sitting, about five feet away from Paul. A few minutes later, I asked Paul if he still had his headache. "No," he said. Then I asked him if he was still tired. "No," he said, a little amazed and confused. All I had done was visualize a beam of blue light flowing out of my third eye and surrounding him. Unfortunately, I did my job too well because Paul had so much energy that he did not fall asleep until very late that night.

The following Friday, Paul and Oss' daughter, Johanna, was scheduled to leave for the southern coast of England with her school class for a week's vacation. This was the high point of her year, and for many months Johanna had scrimped and saved to be able to go. Unfortunately, on the Wednesday night before she was due to leave, she came down with the flu. The next morning, Deborah and I were leaving for Bathe on a weekend trip of our own. Before we went to the station, Oss called and asked us to come by and see if I could do anything for Johanna. We went over to see her, but I was very tired and unable to bring in much energy to help her. I felt badly that I was unable to help her because I knew how important this was for Johanna and how badly Oss felt that she had become sick. But there was nothing more I could do at the time. As we left, I told Oss not to worry about Johanna, that I'd get my batteries charged and send her the needed energy from Bathe. After all, if you can send energy ten feet, you can send it a hundred miles. Distance is no obstacle. I don't think Oss believed me.

That night after we arrived in Bathe, we went to a Chinese restaurant. We were the only people there. While we were waiting to be served, I felt a tremendous surge of energy and started projecting or sending pink light to Johanna. After five minutes or so of doing this, I saw an image of Johanna sitting up in bed, in my mind's eye, and I heard her say, "That's enough, that's enough!"

When we returned to London after the weekend, Paul and Oss told us that Johanna had awaked feeling perfectly fine on Friday. They kept her home Friday as a precautionary measure and then drove her to the coast on Saturday. We told Oss what happened in the Chinese restaurant on Thursday night, but she did not reply. A few days later I returned to the States.

Three or four weeks later, Deborah was at home studying for her final exams. It was a sunny day, (rare for London) and Oss was outside talking to a neighbor. Deborah's window was open, and she couldn't help but overhear the conversation. The jist of it was that on the Thursday evening in question, Oss had been sitting by Johanna's bed while she slept. Shortly after nine, Johanna had sat up suddenly in a deep sleep and said, "That's enough! That's enough!" and gone back to sleep immediately.

This is the story of Barbara S., a business executive who,

at the time of this writing, was located in Alaska. This story is told in Barbara's words.

"*Alan's instructions for using Universal Light to aid in the healing process was a subject that captured both my interest and imagination. The first time I used this method, I thought it was a great theory, but I wondered if it really worked. After several sessions in which the light worked effectively, a rather dramatic situation presented itself which dispelled all my lingering doubts.*

"*My daughter, Laura, was pregnant for the second time. She had previously lost her first child after carrying it for eight months. Seven months into her second pregnancy, she informed me that she would be going into the hospital the next day for a Caesarean section. Recently conducted tests indicated that there was a high count of the same factor the doctor felt was responsible for the death of the first fetus. That night, Laura and I created a meditative state and drew in the light. During our meditation, we concentrated on the baby being healthy, full of life and receiving all the nutrients and love necessary to sustain a normal birth. The next evening when I returned from work, Laura informed me that tests taken again that morning showed the dangerous factor, which had been increasing, now was decreasing at a very rapid rate. The doctor changed his mind. No Caesarean section would be performed. The baby could be carried to term. We looked at each other, and we knew in the deepest part of our being that we had experienced a miracle. We are now mother and grandmother of Larissa Monica, a healthy and wonderful Cherub!*"

This is the experience of Frances C. of Chadds Ford, Pennsylvania, who attended my Wilmington, Delaware, meetings.

"*To understand the full impact of my story, I must preface it with some background. My husband, John, is a staunch Catholic with a scientific background. In other words, anything that cannot be proven or "seen" cannot be real. Metaphysics and spirituality are a threat to his religious and scientific training. Unfortunately, our grown children agree with him on this. However, because of this incident, I feel the door is slowly opening, and they may yet see 'The Light.'*

"Recently (April 1981), John was complaining about his
leg for a week or two. We didn't think it was serious, but it
was painful for him and a concern to us. He had difficulty
walking, and he was in a grouchy mood. At Alan's Sunday
meeting, I mentioned the problem, and he suggested that we
send the healing light to John. He also said that I should not be
too excited or say anything when I got home, but just wait and
see if anything had happened.

"A couple of days later, I asked John how his leg was
because he seemed to be in a much better mood. He said, "It's
the funniest thing. My leg doesn't hurt at all any more. I don't
know what happened.

"I beamed, 'I do,' then I told him what we had done in
meeting. He looked curious but didn't say anything. A week
later our daughter came home for a visit and asked about his
leg. In a loud, clear voice, John answered, 'Ching Li cured it!'
"Thanks to this, there's hope for my family yet."

These next two accounts are the experiences of Cass J., a
teacher from Santa Cruz, California. These experiences are
of a slightly different nature than the ones I have mentioned
so far. They are different because they occurred on a
different dimension or plane of reality from the physical one
which we tend to think constitutes all of reality.

In the second chapter of this book, we talked about the
entity known as Ching Li. While Ching Li is real, he is not a
physical being, but rather a light being. That is to say, his
body is not made up of the physical elements of bone, blood,
fluid and flesh. His body is made up of light and energy.
While he cannot be seen by the physical eye, he can be seen
by the third eye, clairvoyantly.

We now know that, in addition to our physical body, we
also have an energy field, or aura, and generators of
consciousness, or chakras. This is our light body. If we
influence our energy field with positive, higher energies or
inspiring thought and emotions, this inflow will produce a
corresponding uplifting effect on our physical bodies. Our
bodies will actually come into a greater state of harmony and
balance. By raising the energy of our light body, we improve
our health.

When we die, we drop our physical body and shift our

consciousness to our light body. What dimension, or plane of reality we are allowed to enter when leaving the physical body, depends on how much light and energy we have developed while in this present incarnation. On the subtle energy levels, like attracts like. When we drop the physical body, we go to the energy level or plane of consciousness that we have reached through our progress, or lack of progress, in this physical incarnation. Working on ourselves to develop our light body is the best form of social security and retirement stability I can think of.

In this context, death is like the splitting of a seed. When the seed dies, the plant comes forth. Thus, death is not an end but a transition from a limited phase of reality to a greater one.

The astral plane is the dimension of reality closest to the physical. It is an interim plane, or meeting ground, between the physical plane and the higher, spiritual planes. In fact, the Christian concept of Heaven is one of these spiritual planes. There are also dimensions beyond Heaven.

When beings who have earned the right of access to higher planes of consciousness wish to contact or work with us, they often do so through the astral plane. On this level, their energies can exert a positive, stabilizing, healing and inspiring effect on our lives. Ching Li is a being who has gained access to these higher planes but returns to help us by using the astral plane and people like myself who act as his channels. In my meetings, I use part of the time to channel Ching Li for the benefit of all present, and as you shall see shortly, for the benefit of even those who are not present. In addition to Ching Li, many other beings from higher dimensions come through.

The next two examples of Cass J. involve the use of the astral plane. They are in Cass's words:

"On Thursday, March 6, 1980, a Mexican woman with whom I work mentioned to me that she had some strange experiences. When she went into the kitchen early one morning several weeks ago to make her husband's lunch, she heard a voice calling her name, "Maria, Maria Prieta." Thinking it was her husband, she returned to their room and asked him why he was calling her. When he said he had not *called her, she felt shivers and a bad sensation. As she returned to the kitchen, her husband also heard the voice call out her name.*

"At the time she told me this story, incidents of this nature had been occurring for three weeks. During this period of time, their two-year-old daughter awoke each night, screaming, angry and pointing at a 'ghost' until it (the ghost) went out the bedroom door that her parents shared with her. To make matters worse, none of Maria's relatives would come over because they felt uncomfortable in the apartment.

"I told Maria I would ask about her problem in the meeting that night. During the part of the meeting where Alan channelled Ching Li, I asked about the problem. Ching Li first asked me about Maria's children. I said there were two children. Ching Li said there had been another child. I said, 'No.' He then said that Maria had lost a child in miscarriage. This was true. I remembered that she told me about losing her first pregnancy. Ching Li then said it was an astral problem, and he would see if he could alleviate the situation that night.

"The following day, I went to visit Maria. She told me that her two-year-old had slept through the night for the first time in over three weeks. I passed on to her Ching Li's instructions that to keep her home safe from this type of intrusion, she should visualize her house filled with white light each day and imagine her doorway and window filled with lavender light. Maria is a faithful Catholic and is not familiar with light visualization other than the halo so often depicted around Jesus. However, she decided she wanted to buy lavender curtains right away.

"There have been no more incidents since she first told me about her problem, and Ching Li said that he would take care of it."

"One Thursday morning last October (1979), a woman I know told me she was worried about her son. He had gone into a coma that morning after suffering convulsions. I told her I'd ask about it that night at the meeting.

"During the period in the Meeting where Alan channeled Ching Li, I told him (Ching Li) that I was concerned about a five-year-old boy who was living in Oregon with his grandparents and was in a coma. Ching Li paused, then said that it *was due to the boy's feeling of total rejection. When he asked why the boy was with his grandparents, I explained that his mother had sent him there to live just a couple of weeks earlier. She worked full time and spent weekends in another town with her boy friend, returning home Monday morning in time to get to work. The boy was always with sitters. Ching Li then said that the woman was very foolish and irresponsible, and that her first responsibility was to her son, not her boyfriend. He added that no matter what the physical manifestation, the seizures and the coma were due to the feeling of rejection. Ching Li then offered to work with the child later that night on the astral level. The news the following afternoon was that the child had come out of the coma early that morning, and was conscious."*

These are the accounts of Peg S., a former principal and assistant superintendent of schools for Santa Cruz County, California, in her words.

*"My first meeting with Ching Li through Alan was so overwhelming I was cheered, moved to tears, and somewhat bewildered by the wonder of it all. I had to stay away from the group, which I had attended only once, for a whole month in order to integrate the new awarenesses.*

*"What had happened? I had haltingly formed words to express my question something like this: I've been having vivid dreams of my husband who died about six months ago. Are they . . . ? Is he . . . ?*

*"Ching Li answered my half-stated question immediately, 'Yes, of course. He is getting in touch with you. He is all right. He is happy, well and very busy. He would like to be in touch with you more frequently. He is just waiting for you to be open to him, my dear.'*

*"Pause. 'He is a thoughtful man, your husband, yes?'*

*"Oh, yes," I responded, thinking to myself, thoughtful in both ways—very considerate and deep thinking, scholarly man, indeed.'*

*" 'He was a writer, yes?' continued Ching Li.*

*"In our life together, Mac was a frustrated writer turned college professor whose early teachers predicted greatness in his field. His own impatience caused him to burn all of his manuscripts after Saturday Evening Post editors and others*

had returned them for minor rewriting and editing.

"At that first session, Alan/Ching Li told me how to get in touch with Mac more frequently. I followed his suggestion for visualizing the brilliant blue in my mind's eye. It worked! After that, I had many personal conversations with Mac to my great joy and comfort.

"A few months later, I seemed unable to contact Mac easily, reported this to Ching Li, and was told to visualize mint green because Mac had progressed to a different vibration. I followed his instructions and was immediately satisfied with renewed contact and the feeling of his presence. Today Mac seems to be in close proximity or available to me at all times."

(This is also Peg S.'s account.)

"In a question and answer period last winter, I asked Ching Li if it was all right that I had decided not to accompany my twenty-seven-year-old daughter to Australia, as she had urged me to go with her to visit her father's relatives she had never met.

"Ching Li's answer was, 'Definitely. I see her alone having a very moving, important experience. I do not want to say any more.'

"A few weeks later and still prior to her scheduled trip, she came to the group and asked Ching Li if it was safe for her boyfriend to go with her. He responded, 'Of course.'

"I reminded Ching Li of his previous statement about her being alone. He responded that she would have a very moving experience, important and serious, that would not involve her boyfriend much, and he might not understand it or share its great meaning for her, but it was indeed safe for them to proceed.

"Well, the serious, moving experience did indeed take place in a way no one, except Ching Li, predicted. Three days before Heather's and Bob's departure date, we received word that my daughter's young aunt, her namesake, whom she eagerly planned to meet and visit, had been killed in an automobile accident.

"There was nothing to do but proceed with the trip, arriving right after the funeral to meet relatives suffering great shock and sorrow. My daughter felt alone indeed. She was welcomed by and felt useful to the young widower and his *daughter, but indeed went through agonies of aloneness in a strange world of her father's relatives who treated her with varying degrees of affection, disdain and disregard.*

*"She still muses over the learning she acquired through that painful aloneness. Her boyfriend was a comfort but certainly did not suffer the aloneness my daughter experienced."*

This is the story of Shirley O., an artist and head of the display department at Macy's Department Store in the Stanford Mall, Palo Alto, California. These are her words:

*"There was a personal problem at the store where I work that involved the store manager and four other people. His understanding of the situation seemed limited, and I knew of some unjust criticism that he had expressed to others not involved.*

*"He called a meeting for the following morning to discuss the problem. I thought it might be an unnecessarily ugly scene because he was not a person who was inclined to listen or be tactful.*

*"That night I sent light to the situation so that it could be resolved for the highest good of all concerned. I slept that night knowing that it was taken care of.*

*"The store manager was an early riser who jogged before work, arrived before anyone else, and was aggressive and demanding at 8:30 a.m., when most people are still adjusting to being awake. The meeting was set for 9:00 a.m. The four of us were there on time, but the manager was not. We were all surprised that he was late and took the opportunity to formulate what we wished to point out to him and support one another. He arrived at 9:15 and apologized, saying that he had overslept. Because he was on the defensive, he was open to our explanations, and everything was resolved in a few moments of calm exchange. I smiled, knowing it was no accident he had overslept."*

These following accounts are the experiences of the S. family of Wilmington, Delaware. Jere and Sharon S. and their children, Jay and Gina, ages 9 and 12, all attend the Meetings held in Wilmington. Jere and Sharon run their own business, a firm that specializes in interior design for private homes and places of business.

Sharon: "*My first knowledge of 'the light' came through Alan's classes which began in February 1981. I started implementing Alan's principles in my business the next day. I began seeing results in my life immediately. I started by sending pink light to all my clients in all my sales calls. I made a sale to **every** customer. After attending four or five of Alan's classes, our business finished with the best month we have ever had in the five years we've been in business.*"

Jere: "*This represents an increase in sales by almost 1000% over the same month last year. Our overall sales for the first quarter (January to April) are up 30% from last year, and we only started using the light in February. This increase has come despite the fact that we are experiencing a down market in our field.*"

Sharon: "*I meditate every morning now, and use white, gold and pink light. A lot of unexpected, but good things, have resulted from my use of the light. For instance, ever since I've been in business (five years), I've hoped to have an interview in our city newspaper—free p.r. that could be beneficial to our business. In the beginning of April, a reporter from the newspaper called and asked if he could interview me for an article he was doing on home decorating.*

"*Before the interview, I filled myself and the room we were to meet in with pink light. The interview went extremely well. As it turned out, the reporter interviewed four other decorators, but I was the only one whose address he included in the article. On top of that, he mentioned my advice most frequently. We have already started to get results from this excellent and free p.r.*"

Jere: "*In February, I started meditating and surrounding the decorators who work for Sharon and me with pink light. All these women make their own sales presentations to potential clients. Because they are somewhat timid and lacking in confidence, they have not done very well. In fact, they all seemed to average around $900 in sales a month. The first day, I surrounded them in pink light, one decorator had two sales, the first for $900 and the second for $1,600. Another decorator had a sale for $2,400.*"

Jere: *"With all the headaches of running your own business, I often come to the end of the day with many problems running through my mind, making it difficult to fall asleep. The way I've found to detach myself and fall asleep, is to group all my problems visually in the center of my mind. Then I visualize all those problems being surrounded by pink light. This relieves the mental pressure, and I experience a floating sensation. I then quickly drift off to sleep."*

Sharon: *"One day I was feeling so negative that I didn't feel like using the light, even though I know how well it works. That morning I had an appointment with a customer who wanted to redecorate her dining room. After working with the customer for an hour, I realized she had no idea of what she wanted. Losing my patience, I made it quite clear to her that she didn't know what she wanted and therefore was impossible to help. She then left the room to answer the call of one of her children. While she was gone, I thought I'd probably offended this customer and lost her business. With this thought, I started sending her pink light. A few minutes later, she walked back into the room. I had my coat on, ready to leave, when she asked, 'Oh, do you have time to help me with the wallcovering for the bathroom and dressing area?' I then proceeded to make the sale in a matter of moments."*

Gina (age 12): *"This is the third year our school has been integrated by court-ordered busing. My problems started this year. Many of the girls were mean to me. If I was in their way, they would threaten to beat me up. There was one girl, Nickie, who always was picking on me. When I found out about the pink light through Alan's meetings, I decided to use it. The next day (Monday), I went to school and tried it. It worked! Nickie was very nice to me. As long as I used the light, all the girls were nice to me. But when I stopped using it for a few days, they became mean again. Ever since I've used this light at school and things have gone well. I can also send the light much easier now. I've told a couple of my friends who believed me, and they started using the light too. They were very much surprised at the way it worked."*

Sharon: *"One night at the dinner table, I was meeting a lot of resistance from my son, Jay. He refused to eat his green vegetables. I stopped arguing with him and surrounded him with pink light. Suddenly, he stopped dead in the middle of his*

*refusal and said, 'Do you really want me to eat this?'*
   *" 'I sure do!' I said. He then immediately ate the entire
helping without hesitation, then asked, 'Are you happy,
Mom?'*
   *"I was."*
   Jay (age 9) as told by Sharon: *"It seems that since the
beginning of the school year, there was one particular girl in
his class that Jay was having a hard time getting along with.
Try as he might, she was consistently nasty and rude to him.
And Jay would respond in kind. After he found out about the
light and heard our experiences with it, he thought he'd test
this 'light stuff.' In his words, 'I put her in all this pink light,
and pretty soon, she started being real nice to me! She never
acted like this before! Mom, what I want to know is how does
that light work?' Good question, I thought. You don't have to
understand it, just use it."*

   On the evening this chapter was due to go to the typist,
Gina called me to share her latest exploit using "the light."
Since she got me before I took the manuscript to the typist, I
thought her story should be included.
   On Thursday, June 11, 1981, her school was scheduled
to have a mini-olympics. Gina was entered in the girls'
100-yard dash. However, all that week she had had a bad
cold and was worried about being able to compete. On
Wednesday, she asked her dad what she should do. Jere
suggested that she withdraw. Gina did not like that idea so
the next morning (Thursday) before going to school, she
asked her mother, Sharon, what color she should use to help
her in the race. Sharon suggested that Gina use red. Before
the olympics at school that afternoon, Gina shared her
mother's advice with her good friend, Meredith. The two
girls then visualized themselves being filled with red light.
Meredith was entered in the 50-yard dash. As Gina said,
"Meredith isn't a good runner." But that day Meredith won
the 50-yard dash. As if that wasn't enough, both girls
participated in their team's 880-yard relay victory. Not bad
for a lousy runner and a girl with a cold so bad she could
hardly breathe.

   This is the story of Richard, a college student at Foothill

Junior College in Los Altos, California. At the time of this incident, Richard was a student at Palo Alto High School in Palo Alto, California. Richard attended my meetings in Palo Alto on a fairly consistent basis. While he never got around to writing this experience, I remember it quite well and thought it might be of interest to you. I'm sure Rich would have eventually come to write it, but he was always working on his car or going out with his girlfriend or delivering pizzas to earn some spending money. Rather than waiting forever, I received his permission to tell his story for him.

On a Sunday evening, Rich, his friend Bill and their girlfriends, Alice and Joan, went to a rock concert in San Jose. When they got to the arena, they smoked some marijuana before leaving the car. While they were so occupied, they were seen by a police officer and apprehended. They never made the concert, but they did make jail. To get out, they had to call their parents to come and get them. It would be an understatement to say how upset and unhappy they and their parents were about this incident. They were released and a court hearing was scheduled for Monday. They faced a possible fine, a criminal record and a short term behind bars.

The next night, Rich came to the Meeting and brought up his problem. Ching Li was furious with Rich for doing drugs and made him swear to give them up for good before he would even begin to help him. Rich was in a desperate mood and only too happy to agree. Ching Li then told Rich that for the next three nights he was to send pink light to the situation and to the judge so that everything might work out in the best interests of all concerned. He also told Rich he was to do this starting tonight.

Rich protested at this point. He didn't have three nights. He had to be in court the next morning. He had only tonight. Ching Li was adamant. "I told you three nights. I meant three nights."

The next morning, Rich got a call from the court clerk's office. His hearing had been rescheduled for Wednesday morning. That gave him two more nights, for a total of three nights. On Wednesday, he went to court. He was not fined or sentenced or given a record. Instead, he was enrolled in a county program for minor drug problems that met once a week for five weeks. Hopefully, Rich learned his lesson.

Bill is a Professor of Languages in the California State University system. Bill lives in Orinda, California. This is his experience.

"*When I first encountered Ching Li at Alan's Meeting, I felt a little defensive. But one afternoon, as I was starting a customary afternoon nap, I felt his presence in the middle of the room. I felt an infusion of rose light in my midriff and this message, 'I like you much better than you think I do.' I really felt it. For several weeks after that, I got frequent infusions of pink light—really rose light—with flecks of gold, a beautiful shade that has a scent associated with it—that of dusting powder for after a bath.*

"*Then one day last October, I felt it important to take the day off and decided to cancel my classes for that day. The next morning after my first 8 o'clock class, I went into the nearby faculty lounge, feeling remorseful at perhaps having inconvenienced some of my students by not showing up the day before . . . 'What happened yesterday?' I thought. Again, I felt a presence in the center of the room—Ching Li—and he communicated to me something to this effect: 'When you act on your intuitive impulses, this brings instant self-esteem.' Then one afternoon in May, I bowed out of a responsibility, and as I was driving in my car, I felt Ching Lin in the seat next to me, as if he were giving me companionship. He was there for five minutes or so, a long time for him. Several times he repeated to me: 'You need this time to yourself, Bill.' *"

These next three accounts are the experiences or results of three different people who worked with the meditations described in Chapter 10.

Cass, (writing about Meditation Two: Integration): "*As a result of my daily meditation, I have been able to maintain a sense of balance and well-being for over seven months, or ever since I began using Alan's meditations. I enjoy the deep calm and sense of perspective I have gained from meditation. With these new tools, I have gained more control over my life. I can now deal with all aspects of my reality more effectively and confidently. I think the sense of self-acceptance*

*I've gained from meditation is of the greatest benefit to me since it enables me to deal with situations both realistically and more objectively. Before going to Alan's meetings and starting to meditate, I was the victim of large mood swings, feeling first elated, then becoming depressed and cynical. I find that this erratic tendency of mine is no longer a large factor in my life."*

Peggy, a Philadelphia business executive, writing about Meditation 1: Resolution: *Throughout my life, there has been a void that causes me pain and frustration. My father did not love me, or at least, he never expressed his love in the manner I needed. Visits with him were dreaded because he did not respond to the joys or sorrows that were mine or my children's. He only wanted to talk about himself and his needs. He complained whenever I didn't call; didn't visit; didn't invite him—on and on. Guilt became a very heavy weight on my shoulders because I didn't want to call or visit.*

*"This past year, my father became ill. I had to visit. I had to call. And I hated it. During this time, I was attending Alan's meetings and was introduced to the meditation for Resolution. Because I felt so fulfilled in my life with the exception of my father, I used him as the subject for this meditation. Because of this meditation, I no longer feel the pain nor the frustration and guilt. I am able to give him comfort and love. He still cannot respond in the way I would like, but it doesn't matter. I am detached. It's a wonderful feeling."*

Sharon, on Meditation 5. While a businesswoman, Sharon has a deep interest in metaphysics and a strong curiosity to experience her inner guidance. This is her account of using the technique for contacting guidance on the inner, or invisible, planes of reality.

*"Using the visualization process of meditation four, I found myself in a large building with a large portico. It was spacious and sparkling clean with marble floors, white furniture and high, two-story ceilings. I sat down and someone came into the room to welcome me and tell me that one of my guides would soon be with me. Almost immediately, a woman*

*in white, with a white hood over her head, came into the room
and approached me. She identified herself as Sister Marie.
She told me that she would like to give me 'a healing' and that
I could benefit from the vibrations of light blue, the color of the
sky. As soon as she said this, my body became filled with this
color. I could even smell this color blue quite distinctly. The
best way that I can describe how it smelled is to say that it
smelled like baby powder but not quite as sweet.*

*"After I came out of the meditation and returned to
normal consciousness, I could still smell the blue energy. Then
I felt the urge to face into the mirror over my dresser. I was
curious if I would be able to see my aura and the blue light in it
that I was smelling. After a few minutes, I began to see a white
glow around my head and shoulders, and beyond that, a layer
of soft blue around the white. As I continued to gaze in the
mirror, I began to see a bright gold light around my neck.
Shortly thereafter, I realized that the terrible sore throat I had
when I woke up that day was completely gone. I had had this
sore throat for a week. That night I felt a slight scratchiness,
but by the next day, my lingering sore throat was gone."*

Arthur is a chiropractor. His practice was overflowing
and he needed more space. Situated next door to his offices
was a business that was failing. Arthur had learned another
manifestation technique in a course he had recently taken.
For three months, he had been employing that technique in
the hopes that when the failing business vacated the premises,
he would be able to lease the space. However, the owner of
the place had not accepted his proposal. Then he learned the
technique of Meditation Four. He utilized this meditation,
focusing his images at the back of his head. Two days later, he
was awarded the lease.

He was so happy with his results that he shared the
technique with a patient who was having problems finding
the right apartment for herself to live in. She applied the
technique immediately. Five hours later, she received a call
from a realtor she had spoken with for a few minutes several
months earlier. He told her he had an apartment available
that she might be interested in. She went to see it. It was
exactly what she wanted, at half the rent she was paying for
her current apartment.

Naturally, it will not be as simple or easy all the time. By employing these techniques when appropriate, we can, however, save ourselves a great deal of effort, time and wasted energy. We will also considerably increase our chances of achieving our goals.

Usage of the light, through meditation, won't heal all pain or solve all problems, but it can make a large contribution to many areas of your life. Since it's free, easily available and painless, it's a good place to start and a good tool to use to help change, improve or transform your reality.

As the people who have shared their experiences in this chapter discovered, the light of consciousness can often produce startling and wonderful results. There are many more miracles waiting to occur, and those miracles are waiting for you to create them. You are the missing link in the formula of greatness!!

To order your tape cassette of the meditations from *Journey of Love* send a check for $8.00 (per tape) to:

Creative Mastery Programs
Box 26471
Austin, TX 78755

Be sure to enclose your address. Letters about your experience in reading *Journey of Love* are welcome. A list of tapes of Alan Mesher's live Meetings are also available upon request.